WHAT MEN ARE SAYIN

DECODING THE SILENT MAN'S LANGUAGE

CORNELIUS LINDSEY

ISBN 978-0-9964644-2-0 (paperback edition)

ISBN 978-0-9964644-3-7 (digital edition)

For information regarding special discounts for bulk purchases, please contact info@corneliuslindsey.com.

www.corneliuslindsey.com

Printed in the U.S.A.

Table of Contents

Introduction

It is possible for a man to communicate something even when he is saying nothing. Many people may assume his silence means he has nothing to say. However, if they could dive deeply into a quiet man's mind, they would find a virtual blueprint to his communication system. Many men have so much going on in their minds. They just do not know how to communicate their thoughts. My goal in this book is to decode the silent man's language by pinpointing some of the things men deal with and how people respond to them. I understand that each man is different; however, there are significant commonalities among us.

Throughout the book I write about several couples I have had the opportunity to sit and talk with over the years. Today as a pastor, this role has afforded me the opportunity to become well-informed about the silence of men. I have sat with mothers who are frustrated because they cannot get their sons to communicate in a way that meets their expectations.

Most times a wife or fiancée is upset and confused about why her man does not communicate in the manner she thinks he should. She has an expectation, and she becomes frustrated when that expectation is not met.

I had a couple in my office and they were angry with each other. The wife was the one taking issue with her husband. She wanted him to seek counseling because he simply stopped communicating with her. His silence was driving her crazy. She hired private investigators to determine if he was being unfaithful. They found nothing. She tried various other methods to get him to talk, but nothing seemed to work. After what seemed like the longest advisement session I have ever conducted, she threw her hands up in the air and conceded defeat. "Cornelius, I can't get this man to open up and talk to me!" She was upset, and her husband sat quietly with his head down.

I asked her to tell me what she loved about her husband. With some hesitancy, she began to share a few things. She talked about his ability to repair things around the house. She talked about his willingness and ability to provide for the family. She talked about her respect for her husband because of his desire to come home daily and spend quality time with her. She spoke about him being a good father to their two children. She went on and on sharing very positive things about her husband. As she spoke, tears started to stream down his face.

"Why are you crying?" I asked.

"I have never heard her talk about me that way. All I constantly hear is about the things I do wrong. It seemed like she no longer needed me around. I felt like I was a burden," he explained.

There it was. We hit the nail on the head. Her husband was being discouraged with each negative word she spoke to and about him. The final straw that drove him to silence was when he overheard her talking about him to a girlfriend. He recounted what she said in vivid detail. She had never said those things to his face. It angered him that she would divulge such negative detail about him to someone else. It hurt him. Men generally deal with hurt differently than women. This man's response was to grow cold and silent.

Many marriages have dealt with some type of communication breakdown. I like to call it the 99%/1% rule. This principle reflects a spouse's tendency to minimize 99% of all the good things the other spouse does and to magnify the 1% they consider "bad." I understand that the 1% could be substantial; however, I encourage couples to weigh the 1% against the 99%.

A case in point is the couple I just described. There was so much to be thankful for in their marriage. The husband was a loyal, strong, courageous, provider, who was willing to participate in an advisement session to work on their marriage. That choice alone is one that many husbands today reject. The wife was a loyal, strong, confident homemaker with a strong belief in the marriage. She had her flaws as did he, but in the sum total of things they had a really good marriage. Unfortunately, they were blind to all the great things about their marriage and began to focus on the 1% they did not like about each other.

When the 1% flaw is amplified, it becomes huge, and it can lead to divorce. I have met many couples who were divorced because of issues that could have been addressed and resolved. What does the 1% look like? The husband could habitually leave his clothes lying around when he gets in from work. A wife might not be willing to satisfy her husband's sexual appetite. But both may choose to amplify the 1% until it becomes so huge that it overshadows everything good. The couple in question dealt with their frustrations and avoided divorce. Many couples are not that fortunate.

Oftentimes the issues that provoke silence can cause more problems in the household. One spouse is trying to figure out what the other spouse is thinking. This becomes dangerous because one spouse is left to guess what could be the meaning of the other's silence. Most times, a vivid imagination can be totally off base. But there is no way to know the truth of the matter when one person is silent.

One of the biggest issues for the silent man in the marriage I've described is what his wife said and what she did not say. Both are equally important. He wanted to be encouraged for what he was doing right. Hearing words of affirmation or appreciation would actually build a desire in him to do other things right. This type of relational dynamic is somewhat like child development. In order for a baby to grow and mature, the baby has to be fed. For many men, their nourishment is encouragement. Many wives fail to understand this truth so their husbands are malnourished. They are too weak to talk; therefore, they grow silent.

After I asked the couple to discuss what the husband overheard his wife saying to her friend, she apologized profusely. She meant him no harm, but the wound was already inflicted. She now had to work at reassuring him of her love and respect for him. She ultimately ended the friendship with the person she confided in because she realized that "friend" was on a mission to tear down her husband. With a mutual agreement to work on this breach in the relationship, their marriage is thriving today. He has opened up much more. The solution to the problem of his silence was encouragement. It was that simple, yet they were close to ending a salvageable marriage because they had not addressed the troubling 1%.

I have seen many men grow silent because they are not as sexually active as they once were because of a diminished libido or other health problems. They begin to engage in emotional eating and become lethargic. They seem not to be apathetic about life in general. They view their sex drive as a major component of what defines their masculinity. When the instrument between their legs malfunctions, some grow distant and silent. They have encountered a problem they think they cannot fix. The wife does not understand why her husband has become silent. She does not discern that he has lost confidence that he is still strong and masculine without the sex drive he once had when he was younger.

The man's self-esteem has taken a big hit, and his self-esteem takes an even deeper dip when a man becomes self-conscious about the size of his sexual organ. I have spoken with couples whose arguments create great divides when the wives stoop to criticizing the size of their husband's genitals. What these women verbalize is something already in the back of their husband's mind. Some men choose not to respond to the cruel criticism and simply grow silent. Even with an apology after the heat of an argument cools off, a husband will not forget the piercing words of his wife and may actually doubt if the apology is sincere.

Subsequent to an argument like this, sex may no longer be enjoyable for the husband if he feels he cannot please his wife. She could try to assure him that he was pleasing to her, but that would do little for his wounded ego. His silence is a reflection of his disgust in himself, anger towards God, and disdain for his wife. Why couldn't he perform better? Why didn't God endow him more generously? Why did he have to endure a woman he disliked because of her derogatory comments? That silence resulted in a barren sex life. Unfortunately, some of men I have encountered in this situation try to prove their manhood by engaging in sex with prostitutes. This practice gives them a false sense of control and power. These men develop a feeling of dominance and of being in charge as the paid sexual partner fulfills his lustful desires. In reality, these men are not paying for sex; they are paying for power, control, and self-worth.

This behavior of engaging in sex with prostitutes confused me until I sat down with a man who was actively seeking out prostitutes for sex. He explained, "They give me a sense of control and power. I pay them to do something I want, and they do whatever I ask. I am in control, and I like the control!"

I have also noticed how many men view oral sex as an act that puts them in control and gives them a sense of power. They are able to place the other person in a submissive role to provide sexual gratification without having to provide any reciprocal effort at all. These men find themselves on the receiving end of a sexual act that reveals their selfishness.

When a man feels powerless or without control, he can become silent, which is really a sign of his frustration. While he lacks verbal expression; his actions speak volumes. It is important to watch what he *does* instead of listening to what he *says*. A man's silence is best decoded in his actions, not his words. Parents, the wife, the children, co-workers, and his boss are trying to get the man to say something. They fail to realize that he *is* communicating indirectly. He is allowing his actions to speak much louder than his words.

Have you seen a man who struts around like a peacock showing off his assets? He's the same man who shows off his car, boasts about the number of women he has slept with, and brags about the amount of money in his bank account. He flaunts his six-pack, his jewelry, and his designer clothing. He wants everyone to see what he has. He displays his materialism like a peacock unfolds its feathers. This man may not say many words, but he communicates quite a lot in his actions. He is saying, "I WANT ATTENTION! LOOK AT ME! SOMEONE, AFFIRM ME!"

On the other hand, you may see a man who religiously goes to work and immediately comes home. He does his share of household chores; he interacts with the children; has sex with his wife; eats, sleeps, and wakes to do this routine all over again. He lives his life on automatic pilot. His wife craves change, but he has grown distant and silent. She may instinctively judge his communication by what he is not saying instead of judging his communication by what he is doing. He is silently communicating his lack of ambition. He has become apathetic about life. He has lost his drive for adventure. If he is not careful, he will become a miserable man. This does not describe every man in this situation. Some have just become content. The mundane activity represents his contentment, and nothing is wrong with it. The important thing is to watch what the silent man is not saying.

Think about what happens between men and women when they argue. I want to offer a couple of scenarios so you can begin to understand a silent man's language.

When a man begins to feel a sudden rush of excitement about his relationship and a surge of affection for his wife or girlfriend, he usually thinks to himself, "She knows exactly how I feel. I don't need to tell her over and over again how I feel about this particular thing." Many men do not take the time to take a woman by the hand, to hold her, and whisper in her ear.

In the heat of an argument, many men will suddenly stop talking altogether and turn on the PlayStation or camp out on the couch and escape in professional sports. Some grab the keys; get in the car, and drive. Some turn on music. Some go out to the garage and work on something mechanical. Others retreat to their man cave to think.

The goal of this type of man is to avoid confrontation and not become more frustrated. His wife or girlfriend wants to talk about it; he just wants to resolve it and move on. If he can't resolve it, he will retreat until he is able to think of a new plan. Some stop trying to seek a resolution. They just stop trying altogether, and they communicate their desire to stop trying by becoming silent.

For many men, we think in a linear sequence: problem-process-solution. We hear the problem and want to find the process that will bring about a solution. Many men become silent when they do not know the solution or when the process confuses them. They turn inwardly to find a solution. Some women want to hammer away at the problem until they come up with the solution. For many women, simply discussing the problem is the solution. Men become frustrated with that process because they cannot perceive the situation as being solved! They only see it as being discussed. Silence communicates frustration, and a man's actions will show just how frustrated he is. When he gets in the car and drives away, he is communicating that he is frustrated, but does not know how to effectively communicate that to his spouse.

I want to decode several unspoken actions that men are communicating daily. My goal is to provide you with enough information to give you a better understanding of the way men communicate when they are silent.

Chapter 1

Silent Communication

"Actions speak louder than words!"

I heard those proverbial words spoken by a wife to her husband. It was evident that they both were upset. My desire was to help them zero in on the core issue or they could continue being at odds without seeing the root cause. Keeping blinders on about the real problem could mean a premature end to their marriage.

I looked at the wife and said, "Ma'am, your husband is communicating to you in his silence. There is a language he is using that you have not decoded. You are looking for his words, but he is communicating through his actions. You are on the right track. Actions do speak louder than words. Pay attention to his actions."

She wanted him to verbally express what was going on in his heart. He felt talking was meaningless. In his mind, he was taking action. He returned to school, sought the advice of a mentor, took real estate classes, and started to write a book about his life. To him, it was a step in the right direction. To her, it was a plan that made no sense at all. She wanted to feel included in his decisions through constant communication. He felt he was doing all the talking necessary by putting into action a plan, instead of simply sitting and talking about it.

Many men have lost confidence in their words. They assume that since their words do not work, they can speak with their actions. And there are some men who speak better with their actions than they can with their words.

I met a man who could not formulate the words to speak to a woman he was about to ask to be his wife. They had been together for three years. It might be hard for some to understand why he would not know what to say after the woman had been his fiancée for that long. The issue was not his inability to come up with words. His problem, as with many men, was his ability to put those words together in a way that could accurately communicate what was in his heart.

If a marriage proposal was not such a big deal to women, I think many men would hand a woman a box and say, "Here. Put it on your finger! Let's get married!" That seems simple enough. The words may not mean as much as the actions themselves. But the men would look at the actions as being more important than the words.

"Why does it take all of that?" That was the sarcastic question I asked my wife while we were planning our wedding. I felt like the entire day was a joke. I could have gotten married behind a barn with a couple of close family members. I did not think that paying a lot of money for a couple of hours was worth it. We were basically throwing everyone else a party to see us kiss for the first time.

Nevertheless, I did not understand why we could not just get married. We could make it simple, but my then fiancée, did not want simple. She wanted a day to remember. Our arguments about the wedding became very intense. I got to the point where I questioned if we were supposed to be together. I had to fight the urge to ask her, "Why don't you do it all and leave me out of it? I'll just show up on the wedding day!" I have witnessed many men respond like that, but I caution them when I see them headed in that direction. To become silent and uninterested in planning a wedding robs the man of two very important things: (1) the opportunity to enjoy something his wife enjoys and (2) the opportunity for him to develop as a man by doing things he does not feel like doing.

Some men may not say a word, but they may still find ways to communicate their love. The woman may want him to tell her that he loves her. He actually does tell her through his actions. He communicates his love by going to work, taking out the trash, cooking, paying the bills on time, paying for her trips to the beauty salon, buying her flowers, purchasing that dress she's been wanting, taking her out on a date, and going to see her family—even the family members he dislikes. Many feel like those are the things they should do anyway. And in some cases, they are right. However, some men do these things to communicate their love and affection.

I have read and found Gary Chapman's book, *The Five Love Languages* to be quite an interesting read. My wife and I have taken the 'love language test' twice, and our love languages, have not changed. The five love languages, defined by Mr. Chapman, are physical touch, quality time, acts of service, giving gifts, and words of affirmation. My top three languages are still acts of service, words of affirmation, and quality time. Physical touch was dead last on the list for me. However, my wife's highest love language is physical touch followed by quality time and words of affirmation. Acts of service was dead last on her list.

Based on the test, we are exact opposites. While I love the information that is found in the test, I believe men and women have two different communication mechanisms. Tests are not the best measure of communication styles. Oftentimes, men and women change based on circumstances and events that take place in their lives. I have certainly grown to love physical touch, but the test does not show that to be true. While physical touch communicates my love for my wife, I had to explain to her early on in our marriage that my lack of desire to be touched does not mean I am unwilling to touch her. Usually the person who is less interested in physical touch is considered unaffectionate. That is not necessarily the case. I believe affection can be felt mentally as well as physically.

I remember having a very intense conversation with my wife in our first year of marriage. She was upset with me because of my lack of understanding her need to touch and to be close. I did not grow up in a household where the display of affection dominated our interaction, but I accepted her desire to be touched as a challenge for me to mature in that area. I had to ultimately tell her that I was more concerned with touching her heart. My desire is to make a lasting impression by touching her emotionally and spiritually, not just physically.

The challenge of communication between men and women was never clearer to me than when I sat down with a group of men who were discussing their relationships. In the group about half were married and the others were dating. One of the men opened up the conversation by admitting that he was unhappy in his relationship. He and his girlfriend had been together for nearly three years. He started dating her after he ended another relationship.

His current girlfriend was really a safety net to catch him from drowning in his loneliness. She was what many refer to as a relationship on the "rebound." I knew about his situation, and I had given him advice about his previous relationship. But nothing changed. He did not do anything differently. I encouraged him to communicate with her about his frustrations with the relationship. After questioning his motives and actions in his relationship, he said, "Cornelius, I am a coward. I cannot tell her I want to break up." I asked him if he really wanted to end the relationship. He said he did.

Every man in that room lowered his head. They were all going through that exact situation, even the married men. He explained that he felt his girlfriend was emotionally fragile. He said she would not be able to handle him leaving her. We came to the conclusion that he was only speculating. He did not give her an opportunity to actually a reaction to a breakup. He was making an assumption based on what he learned about her in the three years of knowing her.

I asked him if he was continuing the relationship to save her feelings. He admitted that he was making himself unhappy to avoid hurting her. One of the men in the group could not believe that someone else could put into words what he had been thinking for the past six years of his life. He, like the other guy, had a girlfriend who was looking for an engagement ring. Both women wanted to get married to these men and soon. But the men were delaying the prospect of marriage, because their feelings about the women were not sincere. They were too afraid to tell them about their unhappiness for fear of hurting them. They didn't realize they were hurting more than helping the situation.

I asked them if they felt like they would marry their girlfriends, and they both could not answer the question. One of the married men blurted out, "Don't do it! I did it, and I hate my life. Other married men began to agree with the feeling of helplessness and hatred for their situations. The unmarried men in relationships were headed in the same direction. Their fear of telling the truth about their feelings was going to lead to a life of misery. One of the unmarried men said, "I have thought about just going with the flow and marrying her. The only problem is I fear I will leave her at the altar or marry her knowing divorce will be in our future."

One of the married men raised his voice and told him that

idea was crazy. He said it was crazy because he had the same idea. He was in a relationship with a woman he did not really care for. He also said he feared he would leave her at the altar. He stayed in the relationship because he did not want to hurt her feelings. But in the end he chose to settle and be miserable in his marriage instead of being honest and straightforward before they walked down the aisle. I challenged his comments and asked him if he had put any effort into working things out in his marriage. He responded, "I don't want to put any effort into my marriage. I don't love the woman I married."

I asked one of the unmarried men if he felt like he did not have a comfortable environment to tell his girlfriend how he felt about her. He explained that he felt she was also emotionally fragile. He felt like he was beyond talking about it, but he has been too afraid to end the relationship.

All of the unmarried men in the room said they have deliberately done things in their relationships hoping these things would end it. Some cheated with other women. Some started fights on purpose. Others just stopped communicating. But once the fight begins, the men admit their fault and crumble in defeat. They apologize profusely until they get back on good terms with their girlfriends.

Some of the unmarried and married men admitted to being loyal but miserable. They refused to cheat on their wives with another person, but they could not say they were truly happy. I challenged their idea of loyalty. In fact, I do not believe they are truly loyal to their girlfriends or wives. They are really loyal to the idea of monogamy.

One thing they all agreed on was that they were waiting for the right moment to finally end the relationship. They were waiting for the last straw; the big fight; the moment they found out about the cheating; the revealing that someone did something stupid. They were also waiting on someone better to come along. And we know about the idea of someone better. I tend to believe that people constantly think about someone or something better, and this causes many people to run from commitment in relationships. This mindset led me to believe that they were more committed to the idea of monogamy than marriage. Could they really think monogamy was a good thing even though they were waiting for someone better to come along? Possibly so.

Ultimately, they were miserable in their current situations, but it was not enough to send them into the arms of other women. They were intentional about ending one relationship before starting a new one. That sounds great, but they were anxiously waiting for someone new and better to come along that would draw them away from their current relationship. They were waiting for someone or something better to come along. Some of the married men in that room were playing the same game. There were a few married men who were committed to their relationships even though they disliked the women they married.

Another key thing they mentioned was their fear of change. They feared that they could possibly make a mistake by leaving the relationship. They wondered if it was possible for them to leave the relationship but later discover that the person they left was someone they should have stayed with. That haunted them. There was no incentive to leave because they feared the possibility of making a mistake.

All of the men in the room admitted their misery. However, they were unable to communicate it, and some of them could not really pinpoint the source of it. Some thought they were the source of their misery. Others felt that if circumstances were different—better jobs, living situation, higher income—those things would make the relationship better. The fact still remained that they were miserable.

I asked if any of them became emotionally distant on purpose to cause a fight and ultimately the breakup. The unmarried men agreed they were being emotionally distant. They would try tactics like waiting long periods of time before responding to text messages. Some would not answer phone calls. Others would say hurtful things. Many would just get quiet and say nothing. All in all, these girlfriends were suffering and they made to share in the misery their boyfriends felt. The husbands were doing the same thing to their wives. They, too, had become emotionally distant, and their marriages were suffering greatly. They were all physically present, but emotionally absent.

It was sad to hear these men go on and on about their misery. What was worse is they had the power to change their circumstances, but fear kept them from facing the problems head on. They were all willing to do routine tasks like go to work, go home, make household repairs, take her out on dates, bring her flowers, celebrate special holidays, and occasionally have sex to keep their women happy. They were perfecting the art that many men practice—performing out of habit, not out of the heart. They continue in a routine and thus, nothing changes.

Some of the men did not want to leave their relationship because of what they felt they invested in the relationship. They thought about meeting her parents, the awkward moment they met her brothers, and meeting their mothers. They felt they invested a lot in the relationship, and they did not want to think it was all for nothing.

All of the men in the room needed to look at themselves and begin to deal with the issues of their heart. They wanted to make it seem like the woman was the source of their misery. That was not the case. Each one of them had a broken relationship with God. They had abandoned, God, their first love, to find satisfaction and fulfillment in other people and things.

They were finding other things to occupy their time and take their mind off their misery. They were turning to alcohol, pornography, drugs, sports, video games, and anything else that could keep them from thinking about the rotten state of their hearts and their broken relationship with God. Unfortunately, they were using a "love" relationship to fill a void so they would not have to deal with the issues of their heart. The women in their lives became their god and their primary distraction in their relationship with God. They were not in love; they just did not want to be alone.

One of the men started to cry and said, "When my parents

got a divorce I felt like my life was falling apart." He was unmarried and afraid to end his relationship with a woman he really did not love, but chose to keep her around. He was unable to explain why he could not be honest with her and communicate the truth. Finally, he realized what was going on. He was still struggling with the divorce of his parents. He didn't realize that he internalized the issue to such a point where he became a hoarder of people and things. His car was cluttered with stuff that should have been thrown away a long time ago.

He told me about how he was mistreated by people, but he would not cut off the relationships. He was willing to live in misery and constant hurt if it meant that he could cling to the people and things in his life. These are the symptoms of hoarding and hoarders will hold on to someone and some things so tightly that they fail to realize they are choking the life out of the things they are clinging to.

The woman in his life was suffocating emotionally. She did not know what was going on with him. She tried to leave the relationship many times, but he kept going back to apologize. He would do all the right things, but only for a short time. It was not long before he would turn back to his old ways. He would not make any lasting commitments to her. She was becoming convicted about having sex with him because they were not married, but he continued to seduce her. The broken promises and unrealistic expectations of what could be were causing the woman to lose hope.

Both the married and unmarried men had to make some

choices before leaving that room. They had to choose to confront their own issues and humble themselves before God so He could show them their error, heal them of their hurt, and strengthen them so they would never go back to how they once lived. I explained to them that the wounds in their life started like small cuts. They were easily treatable. But the wounds became infected because they failed to treat them. The infection then spread to other areas of their lives. Many of them were suffering from dangerous infections that they never sought to have treated. They had to deal with their wounds.

In circumstances and life choices like these, it is wisdom to seek the guidance of a Christian counselor who is Spirit-filled. I will tell you that journey it is not an easy one. I would also recommend having people in your life who you can connect with, talk to, grow with, and learn from. These people will challenge you, encourage you, and pray for you. Most of all, Jesus must be Lord of your life. That simply means that you confess Jesus Christ as your Savior.

You may recognize that you cannot fix yourself. You cannot solve your own problems. You cannot deal with the issues of your heart by yourself. You cannot stop your erratic behavior on your own. You must have the Savior. You recognize how sin has ruined you, and you see how diseased your thinking has become and how you live because of sin. You realize your only way of escape and true freedom is by confessing Jesus Christ as Savior.

Your confession means you believe He is the risen Savior

who died and rose again that you might be saved by faith in Him. He becomes your Lord when you humbly submit to Him in every area of your life. That means He leads and guides you. He controls your every step. He dictates every event in your life. You seek Him daily. Your life is centered around Him. In fact, He becomes your life. Finally, you believe the Holy Spirit has filled you.

Jesus said to His disciples that He would not leave them alone after He rose to sit at the right hand of the Father. He told them He would send a Helper, and that Helper is the Holy Spirit. He walks with us as if Jesus were walking with us. He teaches us, guides us, comforts us, and pleads the case for purity and holiness. Ask Him for wisdom and direction as you begin this journey, and continue to seek Him. Rely on Him. He will answer you as you call out to Him. Trust Him.

Chapter 2

Hiding From God

My parents never allowed me to live a life without boundaries. They had rules, and I had to follow them. They were firm about me doing what they asked of me. Did that mean I obeyed them? Absolutely not! I was doing everything I wanted to do privately while putting on a public performance of compliance.

When I was young, I will never forget the instructions my mom gave me one morning before I went to school. She told me I could eat anything in the kitchen, but she did not want me to eat the pie she baked for a special event.

My mother's pies are absolutely delicious. You cannot eat just one slice. I have been guilty of eating an entire pie in one sitting. I did not start with the intention of eating the entire pie. It just kind of happened.

I walked in the house from a long day at school and I could smell the pie the moment I walked in the door. I came face to face with temptation. I thought about it the entire day at school. I sat on the school bus daydreaming about it. I wanted a piece of that pie. I had a very serious sweet tooth. I walked in the kitchen and saw my mom's pecan pie. It was a picture of baking perfection.

In my mind, I could hear my mother's voice and her instruction not to eat the pie, but my resolve to honor her wishes began to fade away as I stood there sniffing the sweet-smelling aroma of sugar and pecans--the perfect after school snack. I could have walked away from the situation, but I had no self-control. I started to rationalize that my mother's punishment would not be that bad. In fact, she said not to eat the pie, but she did not say I could not smell it, hold it, and gaze at its beauty. Unfortunately, I had to walk past the pie to get to my bedroom. It seemed like it was calling my name.

The temptation was too strong. I started to rationalize what my mother actually said to me. It could have been that she did not want me to eat another pie. Maybe she was going to make another one. I continued to rationalize the situation until I rebelled. Yes, I ate the pie. I did not just eat one slice; I ate almost half of it. I figured I would get into the same amount of trouble whether I ate one piece of the pie or the whole thing.

After eating the pie, regret and shame set in. I knew what I did was wrong, but there was nothing I could really do at that moment to fix the situation. I continued to watch the clock. I knew my mom would be pulling up at any moment to get the pie so she could take it to her event. Her arrival was like clockwork. I could hear her car coming down the road. My heart started beating fast. My palms were sweaty. I was pacing nervously up and down the living room. I would have given anything to go back in time and to undo the damage that was done.

Every second that passed by felt like eternity. I was afraid to look out the window. I figured she would be in soon enough. I heard her car door slam shut. It was like the final nail being hammered into my coffin. I heard her footsteps as she walked closer to the front door. After a few seconds, I watched as the doorknob turned. She was walking inside, and my heart was quickly sinking because of guilt, shame, and fear of the consequences I would face after she found out what I had done.

Before she walked in, I ran to my bedroom. I knew the consequence was going to be harsh because of my disobedience. All I could do was accept it. However, I was going to make her find me. I hid in my closet. I could hear my mom walk and stop in the kitchen. "CORNELIUS!" she screamed. I knew I was in some serious trouble. I could not blame it on my older sister because she was not home. I could not blame it on my father because he was at work all day. I was there by myself, so my mom knew I was the culprit. I also forgot to pick up my backpack from the kitchen table next to the pie.

She burst into my room and began to search for me. She did not see me because my closet door was closed. She walked throughout the house looking for me and mumbling her displeasure under her breath. I knew she was upset, and the wrath of hell was going to be released when she found me.

She burst into my room again demanding that I come out of the closet. She found me! The gig was up! I had to face my crime. I stumbled out of the closet fully drenched in sweat. My nerves were shot. I knew I was in some serious trouble. My mom looked at me and asked, "Why are you hiding in that closet?" I knew she did not really want an answer. Then she asked, "Boy, did you eat the pie I told you not to eat?" My heart was on the floor at that point. My mouth was dry, and I was about to faint. I opened my mouth and asked, "What pie?" Yes, I had lost my mind, and my mother grew angrier because I was not willing to just admit my wrongdoing. She turned her head to the side, and I knew it was about to be World War III in my bedroom.

Then I said, "Mom, I did not realize that was the pie you were talking about." It was obvious I knew I was wrong, and it was obvious that I knew I should not have eaten the pie. My attempt to hide was enough proof to convict me.

After providing excuse after excuse, I finally confessed to eating the pie. I had to listen to my mother go on and on about obedience. She handed out a litany of chores to be done inside and outside the house. Her goal was to make sure I worked that pie off with heavy labor. After receiving my punishment, I asked my mom, "Well, can I have the rest of the pie since I already ate almost half of it?" To which she made the modest list of chores become severe. I was digging a deeper hole.

That event really ministered to me. I was afraid to be confronted by my mother because I knew my actions were not right. I knew I was disobedient. I knew I should not have eaten that pie, but I did it anyway. Because of my willful disobedience, I ran to escape my mother's presence. I knew her presence meant that my actions would be examined and I would be judged based on my wrongdoing.

I feared the judgment, but I did not fear it enough to stay away from the pie. I feared the idea that my actions would be looked upon and examined justly. Did I commit the crime? Yes. Did I commit it knowingly? Absolutely. One would think that such a bold act of disobedience would evoke an even bolder act of confession, right? Not quite. My bold crime led me to hide away. I knew my only response to my disobedience was either to hide or confess. I chose to hide, and many men are making that same choice in many areas of their lives.

In Genesis chapter three, the serpent approaches Eve to convince her to defy what God told Adam not to do. God was very direct and clear in instructing Adam not to eat from the tree of the knowledge of good and evil. They could eat from any other tree in the Garden of Eden. That was the only one they could not eat from. I want you to picture that scenario. I could imagine that the Garden of Eden was lush with the best of the best because it all came from the Best. Adam could have eaten from anything other tree. That is an illustration of how strong temptation can be to the human flesh. Adam and Eve were not of flesh before they committed this act of wrongdoing. God did not clothe them until after they disobeyed Him and saw their nakedness.

Temptation will cause us to make ridiculous decisions. While I was driving one day, I was tempted to disobey the law. The speed limit on the interstate was 65 miles-per-hour. The minimum speed was 40 miles per hour. That means I could have driven between 40 miles per hour and 65 miles per hour. But the temptation to go above 65 was before me. I saw everyone else doing it. I did not see any police officers around. I did not think I would get caught. What was the worst thing that could happen? So I pressed the gas pedal. I was going well above 65 miles per hour.

As I turned a curve on the interstate, a state trooper was sitting there waiting. He was clocking the cars as they drove by. I knew I was caught. I continued to check my rearview mirror for him. I saw him get in the car and turn on his lights. He was speeding towards my vehicle. My palms became sweaty. I turned my music down—like that was going to help the situation. I was preparing to pull over and accept my punishment. He pulled up behind me, and I started to cross the lanes to get to the median. After I got over, the police officer sped past me. He was going after the car in front of me. I was happy, but I knew it was a wake up call. I needed to slow down and follow the rules or risk having to deal with the consequences. As I started driving, I felt the urge to go speed up gain, but wisdom prevailed.

Temptation came to Eve in the form of the serpent who was crafty in his approach to her. He worked to convince her that she could eat from the tree and not die. It was like my mom's pecan pie. I felt I could eat it and not literally die—though after my mother figured out what happened, I wished I had died. Would I be punished? Absolutely, but it could not be that bad. I felt like the pleasure was more important than the punishment. Oftentimes, a man will base his rebellious actions on the probable judgment. For example, if the man thinks his judgment will not be terribly severe, then he will take the risk of rebellious action.

After Eve was convinced that she would not die from eating the fruit of the tree, she ate the fruit and gave some to her husband, Adam. The pleasure and possible outcome of eating the forbidden fruit overrode the possible judgment that comes from breaking the command. And honestly, many experience guilt and shame for their wrongdoing even though others do not see their actions. They commit a crime without anyone seeing it. But the guilt and shame that results from rebellious actions can eat a person up from the inside out. Their anxiety becomes their judgment.

After eating from the tree, Adam and Eve were both naked. They recognized their nakedness for the first time since they were created. Because they were naked, they sewed fig leaves together to cover themselves. Then they heard the sound of God walking towards them in the Garden. They did something most believers would think is unimaginable even though most of us do it today—they hid themselves from the presence of God. In fact, they went behind the trees so they could hide. Can you imagine hiding from God behind trees?

Adam and Eve, the created beings, hid behind trees, also created by God, to escape the presence of the Creator, God. He is the Creator of all things—including the trees! They wanted to escape being in His immediate vicinity because they knew judgment was soon to come. Eve was convinced she would not die if she ate the forbidden fruit. The pleasure and possibility of knowing good and evil overrode the probable consequence. But reality set in after they disobeyed God and they knew He was coming towards them.

This is the same thing I felt after I ate half of the pecan pie my mother told me not to eat. The punishment did not seem like it would be severe at the time, but reality sunk in after I ate the forbidden pecan pie and my mother was pulling up to the house. Regret replaced pleasure. Like Adam and Eve, I tried to hide from her presence to escape my punishment. And like them, I did not succeed.

They knew their actions were wrong. They knew judgment had to come. God is just; therefore, His judgment must be just and fair. He must give everyone what they are due. As believers and people who profess Christ, we are overjoyed in knowing that our judgment has been extinguished as long as we abide in Him. Nonetheless, Adam and Eve knew God was not going to be pleased with their actions. So, they hid themselves.

Often men will reason about committing rebellious acts based on the possible severity of resulting consequences. I know young men who have gone to prison over and over again. They do not see it as a harsh or a terrible place to be avoided. They believe if the consequence of their actions is not terribly severe, they risk committing the crime again. Prison does not scare them. Death does not scare them. They are not afraid of the consequences so they will risk repeating the crime.

Another commonly held line of thinking is that we may assume that there will not be a consequence because it does not come immediately. We assume that if we can get away with the action, we can possibly avoid the consequence altogether. I have been in that situation where I tried to get away with something I knew I should not have been doing. But I had to ask myself how I could possibly get away with something when God is omnipresent.

I could know an act was wrong, and I would have to close my heart from the truth to keep the guilt and shame from overcoming me. It is one thing to do something and not know it is wrong, but it should bother you when you do something you know is wrong whether you get away with it or not. That truth made a deep impact on my habitual sin. But I did not really stop my wrongdoing. I knew I was wrong.

I would tell other believers about my struggles with sin. There were times when I would cry real tears because of real emotions about real sin, but I was not willing to put any real effort to stopping that sinful behavior I knew God really hated; namely, sexual sin. I would tell people about my "struggles with sin," but I would oftentimes not really express how I was not really struggling; I was giving in to it.

Let's say a thief is trying to break into your house. You are sitting in the living room watching as the thief runs up to your front porch and approaches the door. He attempts to break the lock to gain entrance to your home. You shout loudly to alert the thief of your presence, but he comes in anyway. As the door opens, you toss him down to the ground. He is trying to get away from you, and you are trying to subdue him until the police arrive. You and the thief are involved in a very real struggle. Both of you are trying to gain the upper hand.

On the contrary, you could be sitting in your living room watching as the thief is trying to gain entrance to your home. You notice how he is preparing to knock the door down. Instead of assuming a defensive position, you take off all your clothes, get on your back on the floor and wait for the thief to come in and have his way with you. The difference between the one who struggled and the other who did not was he who struggled was actively resisting. The other had given up and given in. What most assume as "struggling in sin" is actually "giving in to sin." Many men are not willing to stand on their feet and fight against the temptation. They are too busy lying on their backs letting sin have its way with them.

I had a young man tell me that he was struggling with the practice of oral sex. I asked him how hard he was struggling against it. He told me he was fighting as hard as he could. So, I asked him if his sexual partner raped him. He adamantly denied the idea that he was raped. He told me their actions were mutually agreed upon. He was not struggling to the point of death. He was not resisting sin to the shedding of blood. Although he was able to resist his partner's advances, he did not want to do so. I challenged him to finally be honest about the situation. There was absolutely no reason to continue living a lie. Who was he trying to impress by lying? God definitely was not impressed with it. And I was not either.

I remember well finding my way back to God. In 2005, I felt like my life was finally getting on track. I was developing a loving relationship with God. I started with such a desire to know Him more, but that desire began to wane. I loved pornography and sex more than I loved God. I could see and understand the pornography and sex. I did not feel the same way about God. And I did not feel like the consequences of my actions were great enough to make me stay away from the sin.

This eventually led me to stop attending church. I started to rationalize and make excuses for the way I was living. I did not want to sit and hear anything about sin or anything that would interrupt my relationship with sexual lust. I knew I was wrong, but I loved every minute of it. There was only one problem—I could not continue to love it in God's presence. Therefore, I hid myself.

I stopped talking to the people from church I regularly spoke with. I did not want any accountability. I tried to cut off anything that reminded me of God. I put my Bible on the shelf and I was not interested in taking it back down. I did not know what I was going to do, but I did know I could not continue in all the sexual pleasures I was enjoying and then sit in God's presence.

Are you hiding from God?

"Cornelius, I have been in church since I was a little boy," a man told me. "I have heard sermons on everything. I have read the Bible more than once. I sang in the choir. I served as an usher. I tithed on my income."

My response was simple: "If you truly know this then why aren't you living what you've learned? And why has it caused you to become silent? Have you developed a hardened heart towards God? Have you grown comfortable in sin? Are you using certain religious or extracurricular activities as excuses for why you cannot come out of hiding?"

I know that lifestyle well. I used my job as an excuse for not praying. In all honesty, I did not pray because I did not want to pray. I did not want to pray because I was madly in love with my sin. I did not want to part from it.

Even when I started going back to church, I would shut down during the course of a sermon. I did not want to hear anything the preacher had to say. I perfected the art of looking like a good Christian. In actuality, I was using it as a way to cover myself from being exposed as a liar and a phony.

It is my prayer that is not you. If it is, you have to come out of hiding. We have far too many men who are hiding behind the trees! They see the damage that is being done to their families and communities; yet they hide away. They know their silence is dangerous and their inability and refusal to protect and provide for their families is creating more problems than solutions, but that does not stop them. They stay hidden.

We, as the Church, cannot sit back any longer and create a comfortable atmosphere for men to hide away from the presence of God. Join me in praying for yourself and for other men around the world. Let's pray we will encounter our Holy God, be brought to repentance, and be given a burning passion to live righteously in this present age.

Chapter 3

The Wounded Man

I love watching the life of wild animals in their natural habitat on National Geographic. Cameras follow them so viewers can get a bird's eye view of these animals and their actions.

Two of the animals I love to watch are the lion and the hippopotamus. The male hippo is a large mass of rage and testosterone. He controls his habitat with an iron fist. He is very territorial! He will not hesitate to bring a swift hammer of justice if another animal threatens his watering hole. He will fight unto death.

The lion is also a majestic beast. His roar can be heard from long distances. Everything about him is powerful. There is a reason he sits at the top of the food chain. He plays no games. His bite is powerful; his teeth are sharp; the nails on his paws are like cutting blades that rip flesh from the bone. He has a ferocious appetite and must eat often. One thing he does just as much as eating is resting. He rests in the shade during the high heat of the day. He recharges himself with rest and fills himself with food so he is able to protect his territory from other trespassing lions. Like the hippo, he will fight to the death to protect his territory.

One particular episode of National Geographic showed how a lion is able to withstand a near takeover by another lion. I watched the trespassing lion try to sneak onto the lion's territory. He did not get far because of the lion's keen sense of smell. As the rogue lion approached, the defending lion jumped on his feet and ran towards him. The fight was on! They both gave everything they had to bring each other down. After almost an hour, the rogue lion began to step back. His face was battered, his shoulder was badly bitten, and his mane was covered in blood. The defending lion spared his life and chased him off his territory.

As the lion began to come down off the adrenaline-driven battle, he started to limp back to the spot where he laid down to sleep. The camera went in further to see exactly what was wrong with the lion. It was clear that he was injured in the fight. He had a deep gash across his stomach area. He was losing a large amount of blood. The rogue lion used his sharp nails to cut him. He also bit him on his hind leg. Although victorious in battle, the lion was wounded, and he was wounded badly! His fate was inevitable! He was dying a very slow death.

I watched this action unfold from the comfort of my home, but I understood the actions of both lions. The rogue lion wanted a family, so he resorted to taking another's pride. This is a common practice in the lion community.

The lion's pride is important to his overall health and wellness. The lioness is the primary hunter. That is how a lion is fed. The young are born and raised to be ferocious beasts and live out their natural abilities. So, it was important for the rogue lion to have his pride and territory to call his own. Like men, the lion refused to share his space with anyone else. The lion who valiantly defended his pride and territory did not want to give up what he believed was rightfully his. He also knew that another lion coming into the pride would have to happen over his dead body—literally. If the rogue lion took over the pride, he would force the lionesses into submission. If any did not want to submit, they would be killed. And the lion would kill all of the unprotected cubs. This pride and its lineage would be eradicated.

Although the lion seemed to be functional after the heated battle, it was evident that he was not well at all. It only took a couple days for the cameras to return to find the victorious lion lying dead under the intense heat of the African sun. It was not long before the rogue lion returned to claim the pride and territory as his own. After killing the cubs and taking authority over the lionesses, he laid down under a lone weeping willow tree for shade. He licked his battle scars from the war he had just days before.

Watching that entire showcase of ferocity brought tears to my eyes. I could not help but think about men who are wounded. Some have been cut deep by the words spoken to them, wounded by the physical abuse they have endured, and broken by rejection. Wounded men become silent men. One of the surprising things about the lion who met his demise was that he continued in his role as ruler of his pride—even though he was mortally wounded.

This show on wildlife made me think of a married man I knew who was wounded deeply by his mother. The mother abused him physically and emotionally for many years. She would frequently express her disdain for her own son because she had deeply rooted anger and disgust for his father. He told me stories of how she would barricade him in his room so he could not get out. He felt like a prisoner in his own home as a child. He finally escaped the violence and abuse at the age of sixteen. He was forced to grow up quickly. Unfortunately, the streets took him in. He quickly became hardened by life and resorted to violence and thievery to survive. He lived an unstable life, moving from shelter to shelter. He lived in abandoned houses. He sold drugs to make extra cash. He had many run-ins with police. His rap sheet was a long one, but he managed to escape the lifestyle long enough to become something more than just another statistic.

He got his GED, but he could not stop selling drugs. He loved the quick money he got from it. He eventually saw the error of dealing drugs after a drug lord held him hostage. The boss wanted his drug selling territory and money. All of it! Even after giving the drug lord everything, he felt like he was not going to make it out of the abandoned house alive. The boss covered the man's face with a black bag and made him get on his knees. He began to weep thinking his life was over.

He heard the boss ask for a gun. Knowing it would be futile to resist, with hands tied behind his back, he yielded to accepting his fate. In what seemed like an eternity, the boss held the gun to the back of his head and pulled the trigger. The man realized he was still alive—even after what seemed like hours were really just seconds. The gun kept jamming. The boss resorted to hitting the man over the head with the butt of the gun and leaving him there alone on the floor of the abandoned house. He knew his life was spared and he vowed never to get involved in that lifestyle again.

Because he understood the hustle of hard work and entrepreneurship, he started a construction company. He went back to school to improve his craft. After about a year and a half of work, he was making significantly more than he did selling drugs.

In his quest for companionship, he found a woman who became his wife. It seemed like everything was going well for them until his new bride began to chide him like his abusive mother.

His wife berated him and questioned his manhood. She emasculated him with her words. It was depressing to say the very least. When his company was not doing as well, she would tear him down with her words. Not long after they were married, she did the unthinkable. While arguing about a phone conversation the man was having with a female business associate, his wife hit him. When he tried to come after her, she picked up an iron fire poker and swung it at his face, knocking him out.

After finally coming to, he began to remember what had happened. He saw his wife standing over him crying and apologizing for hitting him. He was never the same after that altercation. They both agreed to move past it, but their agreement did not last long. She returned to her mentally and physically abusive behavior towards him. It was too much to handle because it reminded him of all the abuse he endured at the hands of his mother. He turned to drinking and developed low self-esteem. He was emasculated and he became afraid to confront his wife. Her final act that led to their eventual divorce was when he learned she had an abortion without his agreement. Stripped of his dignity and broken self-esteem, he was left deeply wounded.

Like most men, his wounds were unseen but ran deep. I oftentimes hear about men abusing women, but as a pastor, I have become painfully aware of women abusing men. I have had couples sit in my office talking about an abusive woman being the aggressor. Situations occur where emotions got the best of the wife. Unable to restrain themselves, abusive wives can habitually beat their husbands. With this dysfunctional behavior a hidden pattern, the husband keeps his deep wounds hidden. These situations are all too common.

Many wives underestimate the importance of encouraging their husbands. When someone is encouraged, it is like opening up the person's heart and filling it with affirmation which develops courage. The encouraged person is literally being built up. On the contrary someone who is browbeaten and discouraged, that person's heart is emptied of all sense of purpose and courage.

Some men who are discouraged by another words or deeds can grow silent. He may lose all capacity to be vital and productive. He may begin to lose interest in life. He may quit his job or not look for a job. He may make irrational decisions partly because his courage has been depleted. Until he is encouraged, he will remain silent and emasculated. His body will be there with a woman, but his heart may be absent.

I know the wounds brought on by an absent and silent father. The father should be there to affirm his son, uplift his son, lead his son, help his son, and hold his son. His role is to make sure his son knows the right way to go. He leads the path and directs the course. He answers the questions his sons asks and encourages him to live out the good works he models.

The role of father carries significant responsibility. When a father is absent, the boy is left to figure out his own way in life. He seeks affirmation from sexual encounters and other relationships. His absent father is not there to teach him how to think rationally so he begins to think irrationally—usually through sexual promiscuity.

The abandoned son becomes obsessed with the testosterone flooding his body. Clark Kent quickly becomes Superman. The boy does not know what to do with these new physical urges. Jessica is no longer just a girl on the playground. She is not just the girl in the class anymore. She is beautiful and desirable. He cannot navigate those difficult waters alone. He needs a man to help guide the way. When his father is absence, the son succumbs to operating in his emotions. Adding a competitive nature to this becomes a dangerous combination. This young man is never meant to chart his course alone. His father's absence wounds him deeply. There are father wounds that must be healed.

I tend to think the silent father is much worse than the

absent father. I know the silent father; I grew up with him. He is physically present but emotionally absent. He does not talk to anyone, including his wife. He provides no direction at all. What is so discouraging is that he is in the home where direction is needed, but he turns a blind eye to it. He ignores the plight of his family. He refuses to step in and protect his pride from the enemies that seek to overtake his throne. He hides behind the trees and fills himself with surface and superficial happiness.

Looking back on my life, I understand my father's silence. It took me some time to get it, but I understand it now. He was emasculated as a boy. Somewhere along the way he learned to live the way by what he saw. He did not know his father or mother. He was sent to live with his grandmother and uncles. I could only imagine the pain in his heart. I can understand why it could have been difficult for him to step up and be a present and active father and husband. His childhood emasculation could have influenced his attitude. He perfected silence because that was all he experienced. The generational curse of silence had to stop with me. I refused to let it continue as a family heritage. It was not going to happen on my watch.

You recall the lion I described earlier was victorious after his battle even though he was deeply wounded. The wounded beast continued to perform his duties until he succumbed to his injuries. Like most men, he died silently and alone. Before his death, he was seen tending to the pride and even playing with his young cubs. His wound was visible. But he fought through the pain because that was his nature and innate behavior to continue his duties. Many men are doing that today. Although their wounds are deep, they continue to perform duties they feel are their station in life.

My wife and I knew a couple who publicly presented the image of a perfect marriage. From the outside, it looks like they had it all together. I could tell something was not right about the situation. I knew the husband's past. His wounds were very deep. We had discussions about them, but he would never really open up fully to allow anyone to see the depth of his wounds. After a few years of marriage, he was tired of pretending, just as I am sure everyone was tired of watching the pretense. What was hidden came to light.

He went to strip clubs and had multiple affairs with both women and men. Surprisingly, his wife never suspected him of infidelity because they were still intimate on a regular basis. He continued to bring her flowers. He sent her caring text messages. He did all the things to give the appearance of commitment and happiness. He was a great actor. But his wounds were so deep.

With concerns about her health, the wife went to see a doctor. Test results revealed that she was infected with AIDs. Realizing her husband was the only person she had been sexually active with, she was prepared to confront him. She called him immediately after she left the doctor's office, only to hear an automated message say his number had been disconnected. She sped home to confront him and about her diagnosis. She opened the garage to see his car was gone. She walked in the house to find all of his things were gone as well. None of his belongings were left behind. The fact was he learned that he had AIDS a little over a year before she discovered she was infected. He did not tell her. He just kept playing the role dedicated husband.

Another husband I encountered was also in hiding, but his issue was infidelity with another woman. The negative things spoken to him throughout his life wounded him. He felt inadequate as a man and a leader. He could not keep a stable job. Most of his work was seasonal. His wife had a successful career in banking. She earned more money than he did and that did not sit well with him. His pride was deeply wounded because of it. After nearly seven years of marriage, he began to drink to mask his pain. He found comfort and peace in a whiskey bottle. He and his wife soon separated because of irreconcilable differences. His drinking led him down a dark abusive path.

There are usually two things I see in a wounded man. They are: a desire to self-treat his wounds by filling a legitimate need illegitimately or a tendency to cover the wound.

Oftentimes, men try to treat their own wounds. They realize they are hurt by the things that were said to them by those they loved. They cringe when something or someone reminds them of a family member who abandoned them. They have the wounds to show their injury.

When I was young, my mother told me not to touch the hot stove. She warned me over and over again. But it seems her warnings made the temptation to touch the stove more attractive. The temptation was too great; I touched the hot stove. I still have the burn mark as evidence of the wound. And there are other less visible wounds. I still have the wounds from being bullied and talked about when I was younger. I still have the wounds from my silent father. Like many men around the world, our wounds run deep.

Sex, drugs, money, power, and influence become the medicine that some men use to treat their wounds. Alcohol helps them to remain numb so he does not have to think about the pain that came before the wound. I know about pain. When I touched the forbidden hot stove, I felt the pain long before I noticed the wound.

Drugs help to reduce the thoughts and numb the pain. Many take the bait of the enemy to fill a legitimate need illegitimately. We have a legitimate need of peace, acceptance, and masculine identity. We are able to legitimately fill those needs through Christ and our earthly father or a male influence.

When we lose confidence in our earthly father and do not fully understand the affirmation we can attain through Christ, we turn to counterfeit solutions. Those substitutes for authentic affirmation provide temporary enjoyment that does nothing to curb the intense pain and heartache looming beneath the surface. What develops is a love or the feeling of relief. Once men realize that mere relief is temporary, they will search for it again and again and again. This kind of relief is never lasting.

Marijuana is another choice of the stressed out man because it provides a temporary relief from pain, but the numbing effect wears off. He gets to the point where he cannot stop seeking the temporary relief even if what he is seeking destroys him.

The late night escapades with random women or men bring temporary relief, but after the sexual pursuit ends, he runs back to find someone else to sleep with. He jumps from person to person. He goes from one X-rated site to another one in search of something to fill his lustful desires. Over time the lust begins to grow more and more until he is involved in full-blown perversion. This is when his guard is let down so low that he no longer has any standards. It doesn't matter to him if a woman or a man is satisfying him; all he cares about is his lust being satisfied and his wound being temporarily treated.

His guard is down so low that he fails to recognize the danger of his ways. He is killing himself, but he does not realize it. He thinks he is treating his wound. In actuality, he is infecting it with lustful poisons. Some men get to a point where they know their illegitimate void fillers are killing them, but they do not care.

Patients are told that it is important to deal with a wound quickly before infection sets in and spreads. If infection spreads, more radical treatment is necessary. It is like gangrene which can lead to the need for amputation. Early treatment could prevent such radical treatment.

Indulging in sex, drugs, overeating, and other illegitimate void fillers are like infection. These things keep hidden wounds from being healed, but functions like a band aid keeping the wounds covered. The biggest problem with self-treating the wound is that, most times, we do not know what we are doing. Have you ever tried to self-treat a wound?

My parents warned me about not playing near a shed that

had collapsed some months before. A tornado had come through and knocked the shed down. It crushed everything under it. There was glass and all kinds of debris under it. I wanted to jump on the top of the shed. I slipped and cut myself. It was not really deep, but I felt like it was serious enough for me to go inside and treat it.

I tried to hide the blood from my parents. I ran through the back door straight to the bathroom. I watched my mother administer first aid to my wounds for years. I noticed she always poured alcohol over the wounds. I thought I should use the same method that she did. Yes, I was preparing to pour alcohol all over my wound. Did I realize the amount of pain I was about to experience? Absolutely not! But, I did it. I screamed like someone had cut off my arm. The pain was intense!

My mom ran in the bathroom to see what happened. She saw that I cut my arm and I was pouring alcohol on it to treat it. She looked at me and said, "Son, you didn't need to do all of that. You should have just used some of that first aid cream I have in the cabinet. It would have been just fine." I could not believe that I went through all of that pain when the treatment could have been much simpler and a lot less painful.

I did not know what I was doing. I did not know how to treat my wound. But I did not want to ask for help. I chose to risk horrendous pain than ask anyone for help. Many men have that problem. I know because I used to be one of them. Instead of asking someone for help, I tried to act like I knew what I was doing. You do not have to perform the operation alone.

Whatever is covered will not get healed. The bandages help to keep dirt from getting into a wound. However, it also discourages the wound from breathing, which ultimately helps heal. If the wound does not breathe, it will not heal. It slows down the healing process.

I want you to recall all the wounds you have in your life right now. In fact, I want you to go a step further than just remembering them. Get a sheet of paper and write them down. Use more than one sheet if necessary. It could be hurtful things your mother said to you. It could be the hurtful names your wife called you. They are those things that are said in the heat of an argument. It is when your past is used against you or any of your mistakes are constantly thrown in your face. It is when he uses your past mistakes as evidence of why you will never be worth anything.

Be honest about your wounds. Covering them up will not help you. Your silence does not help you. Writing down your wounds is a major step. These things are not easy to say or write. The fact that you did is powerful and pivotal. Confession, the willingness and ability to be open and honest, helps the healing process. You are healing! You ripped the bandages from the wounds so they could heal.

Contrary to popular opinion, men can be raped also. Men are given the date rape drug and sexually assaulted by aggressive women. Some men are seduced to perform lewd sexual acts. In fact, the bars and strip clubs are all designed to be places of seduction and false ecstasy. The strobe lights, fog machines, sensual music, alcohol, dancing women, and other elements all work together to create a seductive environment that lures men into taking out their money, freely giving it away, and throwing caution to the wind.

A man can go from paying to watch a seductive woman to paying to have sex with her. The force driving him is not physical; it is emotional. He takes the bait, and she has her way with him. He is intoxicated with lust and no longer sober-minded. Did he make the decision to walk into a strip joint on his own? Definitely. He knew what he was doing, but the sensory allure of the scene got the best of him.

Your wound could be physical abuse at the hands of a parent, guardian, sibling or spouse. I have known many men who were being abused mentally and physically by their spouses. The woman, who looked like she could not hurt a fly, was beating her husband into the ground. She might even taunt him to hit her back with the ploy of having him arrested. She might criticize his sexual performance, causing him to grow silent. This abuse is very real.

Your wound could be an absent or silent father. It could be a disengaged father who was not involved or concerned about any aspect of your life. Or it could be because your father was in the home, but made no effort to teach or affirm your manhood.

Maybe you were bullied as a child. I know how that feels. As a child I was short and pleasantly plump. I could not eat my lunch in peace without someone coming over to steal food from my tray. When I was a freshman in high school, there was a senior who would steal my cookies. He would take off running around the cafeteria. When I chased after him to get my cookies back, I realized everyone was laughing at me, which was regular the humiliation I suffered.

If you ever attempted to compete for something and lost, that loss could have left a wound. I remember running for a position in high school as an extracurricular activity. Out of all the candidates in the campaign, I came in second place, but that was last place in my book. In my mind, I should have won.

I will never forget the winner's campaign slogan: "Keep It Simple Stupid." My feeling was that she was the choice of the advisors, not the students. I asked for a recount, but it was not granted. That was a difficult pill to swallow. It was my first major loss, and I took it really hard. It was a wound for many years of my life. Because of the loss, I questioned my ability to win other elections. I eventually overcame that fear and won every election I ran for from that point forward.

Wounds don't have to be inflicted from major incidents. Nothing is too small. You could hate the way you look. I empathize with you, too. I rarely took pictures because I believed the bullies. I believed they were right about me. Maybe I was not attractive or too fat to ever be in a relationship.

I met a young man who was born with a physical deformity. He only had one arm; the other was a short stub. He also had a cleft lip. He told me about the looks he received from people. He told me how much he hated God for making him that way. He was buying into the false idea of "normal." He wanted to look like every other man. I looked him in the eyes and said, "Brother, every man has a different look. Not one of us is exactly the same. Embrace your differences." I pray you do the same.

Treating a wound is important and equally important is not leaving wounds over-exposed. You want to make sure nothing gets inside of the wound to cause unnecessary infection. I strongly suggest that you be selective about who you share your wounds with. Not everyone has your best interests at heart and some may even use your wounds against you.

Consider getting an accountability partner. This is another man who can hold you accountable for your healing process. Your accountability partner is like your best friend or a wise advisor who knows you well. Don't return to the superficial void fillers. Stay the course. It's time for you to be healed.

I would recommend your accountability partner be a man who is a loyal follower of Christ and who is filled with the Holy Spirit. It is important to have someone who is saved and filled with the Holy Spirit so he can constantly lead you back to the truth. He can redirect you to the Great Physician, who is Jesus. Ask your accountability partner to pray with you and for you. Ask him to challenge, encourage, and regularly check in with you. This man covers you and your vulnerabilities so others do not hurt you during the healing process.

The worst thing that can happen is for someone to come and throw salt on one of your open wounds. Your accountability partner makes sure that does not happen. You could have your men's ministry at your local church keep you accountable. It could be a group of your friends from school. Reach out to your pastor. It does not matter. Just make sure you are in a place where you can comfortably confess and expose your wounds so they can properly heal. Just know that you do not have to do this on your own. In fact, it is not good for man to be alone.

Chapter 4

The Walking Dead: Spiritually Dead and Mentally Exhausted

I recently watched parts of a movie on television about dead men and women walking around trying to kill the living. I missed the part that explained exactly how these dead people rose from their graves and the reason for killing the living. The concept was rather interesting, nothing more. After watching those who were living fight off the walking dead, the Holy Spirit began to deposit some things in me that shed light on the current state of men which reflects the premise of the television show I watched.

Two groups exist in our world today. One group is the walking dead and the other is living. Sadly, the group that represents the walking dead is much larger than those who are living. When I write about the walking dead, I am referring to them being spiritually dead. We emerge from the womb with an inclination towards evil. Because of Adam's transgression when he disobeyed God in the Garden of Eden, we are born into this world with sinful desires. We have the ability to know good from evil. That knowledge has been made available to us since Adam ate of the fruit from the sacred tree. Because of our fallen state, we are in need of salvation.

We are like men trapped in a burning building. In fact, we are born in that burning building. The only way we escape is through the door that leads to peace, freedom and eternal safety.

While inside, our eyes are opened to the way out of the burning building. We see the danger of the fire. Getting out is crucial to our survival. The flames are intensifying, and the heat is rising. The building could become quickly engulfed in flames. It could happen in the blink of an eye. The person entrapped in a burning building may realize that time is running out. As he races around looking for an escape, his vision may be impaired by smoke and debris. He might even stumble over others who do not have the desire to find a way to safety.

A man trapped in a burning building might hear a voice yelling directions for a way out. There is urgency in the person's voice. Compassion is clear in the volume of his voice. Dazed and disoriented, the man in the burning building might perceive other people standing in front of many doors that could provide an escape.

The persistent call of the first voice seems most convincing. You see other doors all around you. Men and women are standing in front of those doors telling you to try their door.

You run from the first door where you felt the passion and conviction of the man's speech towards another door. The man in front of it is convincing. You go to open the door, but you recognize so many irregularities with it. You have no true conviction about it. And you cannot get the first door out of your mind.

After trying many other doors, you hear the faint cry of the first man yelling for you to go out the beaten and battered door you stood in front of before. "Come on, brother! Go through this door before it is too late! This building is about to explode.

Nothing will be left. None who are left will be saved." You cannot ignore the message any longer. You are compelled to run out the door, so you do it. You immediately have a sense of peace.

While you are outside you have a very strong desire to run back in and tell others about the way out. Your family and friends are in that building. You can see the fire and the smoke. Many of them are trying to navigate their way out, but they are trying every door but the one that leads to true freedom. You race back inside and stand beside the man preaching salvation and redemption. You run back into the rooms where people are dancing, fornicating, drinking, and dishonoring the sacrifice of Christ. You want to tell them about the way out. You are wiling to risk your own life for their eternal salvation. You recognize that preaching will cause them to know the truth, so you preach with passion and conviction.

Any man who does not go out the door will not be saved. Brother, the door is Jesus Christ. You must confess Him as Lord and Savior. He quickens you with new life! Leonard Ravenhill, a true preacher of godliness and salvation has said, "Christ did not come to make bad men good; He came to make dead men live." And men do not come alive until they have confessed Jesus as Lord and Savior. Have you made that confession of faith? If not, I strongly urge you to do so. Open your mouth and tell Jesus that He is the way. Tell Him you recognize your sins, and ask Him to forgive you. Ask Him to fill you with the Holy Spirit so He can lead, guide, protect, and teach you. Confess Him right now.

If you have already made that confession of faith, then you understand what it is like to escape the burning building. You have experienced the peace that comes with salvation. If this is the first time you have ever called upon the name of Lord, then welcome to our family of faith. You are no longer a dead man; Christ has given you new life. You have come alive through Him. Now, live!

Men have many issues facing them, but the biggest problem we have is the deadness of our heart and the ignorance in our thinking. Christ must quicken a dead heart. Afterwards, the mind must be renewed. If it is not, it will not grow. An idle mind is not just the devil's playground; it is a desert. We men must educate ourselves.

The process of education is like planting seeds in the ground. Each seed that is planted has the ability to be watered for growth. Our ability to act on the truth we know is the watering process. I have heard countless people say that knowledge is power. That is not necessarily true. Knowledge without proper application is unproductive. Knowledge is not meant to lie dormant; it must be applied and acted upon if it is going to produce real power and bring real change.

I oftentimes tell my testimony of my faith walk with God. I was a sophomore at the University of Georgia when I started to really get serious about my faith. Those were some of the loneliest days of my life. I wanted to hear the voice of God so bad. I wanted it more than anything. I spent hours in my apartment in prayer. I listened to sermons all day long. I studied the Bible as much as I could. I spent a lot more time in the Word of God than studying my textbooks.

My passion to achieve my goals and do what I wanted to do was dying away. I was dying to my selfish ambitions, and it was a good thing. The Lord was doing a serious work in my heart. I needed His help and I needed to know that He was with me. My book, *So You Want to be a Man,* tells the full story. After being in the presence of God for what seemed like forever, He spoke to me. I believe He told me to leave college and truly depend on Him for my successes. I did just that. I did not turn around. I kept going forward. I eventually dropped out of college, moved back in with my parents, and started a journey of faith that many doubted was true. Although it was difficult, I look back and I am thankful that I dared to believe I had heard from God.

Many hear or read my story and automatically assume I do not believe in education. That is far from the truth. I was fully prepared to get my degree. I planned on becoming an attorney. But my ultimate goal was to run for political office and remain in office until I retired. I wanted to serve my constituency. That was my plan; however, it was not God's plan. He desired for me to preach His Word, pastor a church, and much more. I had to submit to Him. I did not see it at the time, but I had to be willing to walk an unchartered path and believe He was there with me.

I have never been one to marginalize the power of knowledge and education. I have my fair share of criticism about the way it is packaged and delivered today. It has become a big business, but that does not mean I am against learning. After dropping out of college, I read most of the textbooks I purchased for my classes. I did not need a teacher threatening me with a quiz to actually read the text. I was fully capable and responsible for reading it on my own. I did not allow being out of college hinder me from learning. I fully intended to learn and continue learning. My focus was not on a diploma four years down the road. I was focused on life-long learning. I started learning for life, not an exam. I needed to retain the information so I could continue to mature and be better.

I am a firm believer that our society is a graveyard where potential is laid to rest. The human mind has the capability of retaining so much, but we fail to sit down long enough to read, grow, and apply. Television shows, sport channels, and video games have captured the minds of our young men. Many have a difficult time thinking critically. I come across too many young men who do not know how to do very basic things. They all have different excuses as to why they cannot perform simple tasks. In all honesty, their problem is simple; they do not read.

I believe that leaders are readers. I love walking into some of the homes of men I respect in business and ministry. I walk into their offices and I see volumes of books. These men do not show me their collection of televisions. Instead they show me their collection of books. One mentor I had years ago, walked me into his personal library. There were literally thousands of books. He had every book I could think of. I asked him if he read all of them. He said he read most of them. I put him to the test. I started pointing at books and asking him to tell me about them. He did not miss a beat. He passed my test with flying colors. I was shocked, but I had no reason to be.

He was able to tell me so many things I did not know about random things. His primary field of study was dentistry, but he could tell me about mountains, animals, food, bacteria, and so much more. He knew a little something about everything. It was wonderful to experience.

This avid bibliophile told me about his upbringing. It was not the best. His father was absent, and his mother was a high school dropout. She could barely read. She did everything she could to make money and provide for her family. He told me about the people he grew up around. It was truly sad to hear. I asked him what he believed separated him from everyone else. He said, "My mother made sure I could read. Then, she made sure I read often." He did not grow up with the best toys or clothes. His mother invested in books. He got books as birthday presents. He got books for graduation gifts. His mother made sure he had books. And the knowledge he had in so many things proved he was truly a reader.

He refused to be another casualty in the graveyard of potential.

There are two main things I want to encourage you to do to make sure you are not counted among the walking dead. The first is to confess Jesus Christ as Lord and Savior.

The second thing I encourage you to do is read more. Never stop learning. It is important for you to read, and it is just as important to make sure you are reading the right things. I encourage you to read the Bible. I always encourage beginners to start with the Book of John. Then, read Matthew, Mark, and Luke. Then, go to Acts and read it throughout. The Old Testament can be tricky to navigate. Do not be afraid to dive into the Word. Pray and ask the Holy Spirit to teach you as you study. I also encourage you to read books on leadership, business ethics, communication skills, and relationships. Have it in your mind that you are going to grow and keep growing.

You can escape the burning building through Christ. Just make sure you do not remain stagnate once you get outside. Read and read some more.

Chapter 5

On the Backs of Men

There are many expectations that have been placed on the backs of men. These expectations have brought some of the most renowned men to their knees. Their backs have been weighed down by standards that God have not assigned to His sons. These are things like having to purchase the biggest and best to keep the family happy, displaying the largest ego in the room to prove his superiority, the need to be physically tough to prove his physical dominance, and so much more. I am convinced that our men are not silent because they choose to be; many are silent because they are tired.

I know what it is like to be tired. I oftentimes grow weary even in my well doing. I look for a strong shoulder to cry on and hold me up. As boys, many of us are told not to cry. We are told not to express our emotions. Trying to bottle up all of those emotions causes us to grow weary from the stresses we carry inside of us.

I remember some years ago when my wife received some

bad news. Her nephew committed suicide. I had just seen him a few months before. I had an opportunity to sit down with him and speak with him about his life. It was a great conversation. I did not think it would be our last.

As my wife cried, she crawled into my arms so I could hold her. So much bad news weighed her down. The death of her nephew, the miscarriage of our first child, and the death of one of her friends—all of this was a lot for her to handle. She found safety in my arms. She found strength in my arms. She found love in my arms. I held her close until she went to sleep. I put her in the bed so she could get comfortable. I rolled over to my side of the bed. My heart was heavy. I began to think about my own emotions.

I began to question what I was supposed to do in my moments of weakness. Where was I supposed to turn for comfort, safety, strength, and love? Whose arms could I run into so I could just go to sleep? I am my wife's symbol of strength. I am the leader—he who must be courageous and mighty even though there are times I want to be vulnerable and remove the mask of strength. I did not feel like I had the option to mourn. I was not afforded that opportunity to be vulnerable and climb into the strong arms of another. I needed to be strong while my wife was able to freely express her heart. I had to rest knowing that Jesus was my strength, and my heart truly breaks for men who do not know this truth.

Men are usually expected to perform at all times. Men are expected to be strong at all times, show no emotion, communicate effectively, fix everything, protect everyone, and so much more.

To live up to these lofty and unfair expectations, men begin to identify their value with academic degrees, money, public acclaim and much more. But how would you react if I told you men get tired from the heavy load of responsibility we carry on our backs? How would you feel knowing that we get lonely and resentful because of the weight of other people's expectations of them?

We struggle at articulating our feelings because we have lost confidence in our words and many of us lack the ability to share what is in our hearts. We grow tired from being the rock for everyone else. We desire to lean on a tangible rock while having faith that the Cornerstone will not let us fall. Whose shoulder do we turn to and cry on? Where is the safe place to share our hearts, our insecurities, and our ailments?

Many do not understand the danger of being tired. When you are tired, you can become irrational. This is why it is important to never make a decision when you are tired. You do not see or think clearly. To be a tired leader is even worse. This means you have been tasked to govern and guide, but you are irrational in your decision-making because you are worn out from suppressed emotions, wounds that have not been healed, and the obligation to be the backbone for everyone and everything else.

Many say men play games. Unfortunately, society emphasizes the need for the boy to perform. Men have learned from watching and playing games that one must keep score and the more points scored, the bigger the win. For many men, it is not just a game; it is a report card. It is a report that follows the guidelines: the greater the performance (more sexual partners, money, etc.), the higher the grade. Society rewards men based on their performance more than the content of their character. If men were rewarded on earth based on their character alone, many bank accounts would be empty and award shelves would be bare. This is why we cannot expect a perverse player to play a clean game.

The demands placed on the back of men are not an excuse for us to refuse to fulfill them. However, there must be fair expectations in the fulfillment of them. Older women outlive men because many of us go to our graves without ever asking for help. We would rather die trying to appear strong than live admitting we are weak. Many men see death as an opportunity to escape their reality. It is their opportunity to release the heavy load without appearing weak.

It could be that the men in your life are tired. Their irrational decisions—especially around their mid-years—could be because they are worn out and exhausted from the demands of life. This could be reason a man is a 51-year-old chasing a 23-year-old and testing out his new motorcycle on the road with friends. He probably feels like he is able find life outside of his routine activities. He divorces his wife of 27 years to discover himself. In some cases, he tries to reinvent himself outside of his normal responsibilities.

My father and I have not always had the best relationship; however, it has improved over the years. I am very thankful for that. One of the things I respect about my father is his work ethic. He will work, and he will work hard! I can count on that from him.

I have seen him work very hard to make sure money came into our household. Watching his work ethic inspired me to work hard as well.

I started working at fifteen. I paid for my first car with cash and experienced the excitement that comes with working hard and not having to ask anyone for help. Unfortunately, like my father, I learned to perfect the kind of independence that walls people out. This is something most men suffer from today.

I have watched my father for years deal with health issues, but it has taken me many years to finally pinpoint the larger issue—his silence. I can tell that he is weighed down with responsibility. He desires to be the leader of his home and bring in more money. His desire has led him to have multiple jobs just so he can say he is making more. Some will say it is just an ego problem, and I would not disagree with them. However, we must realize that society has placed men in that predicament. And we must understand that men have a natural drive for achievement, fulfillment, being fruitful, abounding, and conquering. God calls no man to be lazy.

My father developed a very serious alcohol problem that has led to some serious illnesses, but he refuses to ask for help. This could be because he does not think he needs help. He takes that same silent approach to his health. Instead of including his family in his health issues, he manages on his own—and silently.

He is eroding before my very eyes, but he does not say a word. It is a slow decay. His body does not function as it once did and his stamina is not what it once was. He still wants to retain the spot as alpha dog, but his body is working against him. The doctors give him more bad news and find more complications. To avoid hearing the news, he stops going to the doctor. He does not take the medicine because he doubts it will work. He wants to fix the problem alone. And, like many men, he has all but given up trying to fix the problem. Instead he is living out the last years of his life doing whatever he wants to do.

A young man I mentor has experienced a few bumps in the road. Overall, he is a good kid, but his attraction to drinking hard alcohol works against him. He looked me in the face and said, "I don't have a problem, Cornelius." When he told me about the number of drinks he while watching a game with friends, I begged to differ with him. I asked him who drove home. He drove himself. Yes, he was drunk. After bringing the danger of this issue to his consciousness, he broke down.

He did not realize how serious his abuse of alcohol was becoming. He was not just putting himself in harm's way; he was endangering the lives of others because of his reckless behavior. Drinking began as a way of drowning out his problems and avoiding the issues of his heart. Drinking was his escape from reality. It was his drug of choice.

Is it true that men are purposed to lead? Absolutely! Adam was created before Eve. This suggests the order of headship; however, the head is not meant to be silent. His physical structure is built to handle much more than the woman, but the load—even for the strong man—is enough to weigh him down and render him ineffective. A heavily loaded back cannot help but become bent, and a bent back limits one's ability to see where he is going.

I have heard of men dying silently in their living room, lying in their beds, outside in the garden, or slumped over their desks. It seems fewer die in a hospital room. On the other hand, I frequently visit women in their hospital rooms where they are receiving care and asking for help for their illnesses. Why are the men not going to ask for help? Well, many of us do not want to ask for help no matter how bad the situation gets. We would rather die carrying the load than risk being vulnerable. For many, the idea of asking for help is a sign of weakness, and men do not want to be weak.

The thought of not asking for help or being vulnerable sounds foolish when you think about it. But the root of the issue is pride. While some see pride as a terrible thing, it does not have to be. It is honorable to take pride in your work, your appearance, and your words. It becomes dangerous when pride tries to usurp the authority of God and disguises itself as false humility. The Holy Spirit helps to draw the thin line between pride and humility. He will lead us so we do not live as prideful men. Instead, we properly take up our calling, deny ourselves, and follow Christ.

Being vulnerable is not always easy. I know from experience. As I stated in the last chapter, an exposed wound has the greatest risk of being infected. However, if it is not exposed it will not heal.

I knew a young man who had a very deep secret. Like most of us men, when confronted, he danced around the secret. He came to my office wanting to be transparent, but he was hesitant.

He could not help but think about what would happen if he told me the whole truth. He wondered if I would look at him differently. He was not sure if I would accept him or affirm him because of his actions. He wanted help, but he was too afraid to be completely open. After almost two hours of talking around the issue, I looked him in the eyes and told him to tell me what was going on. He bowed his head and tears began to flow from his eyes.

What he did was dangerous and damaging, but instead of emasculating him, I reached over and hugged him. Later he told me that was the first time he had a chance to be open and confess what was in his heart. That was the first time he did not have to be strong for anyone else. That was the first time he had a shoulder to cry on. This freedom and safety to be open led to an even lengthier conversation. He left my office with a sense of freedom from his past. I am proud to report that the young man is now married. He is enjoying his faith walk with the Lord. He is a different man. He is God's man. He finally released the weight of the world and the weight of his past from weighing him down. He allowed the act of confession to start the healing process. I recommend the same for you.

Instead of carrying that heavy load of responsibility on your back, I encourage you to cast it on God. That means you trust that He is with you. I understand that the bills are still due, your family still has to eat, and things still have to get done. This does not mean you become lazy and expect God to do everything. You work hard to make sure He has something to work with.

Noah was told it was going to rain, so God gave him

instructions to build an ark. God used what Noah built to fulfill His promise. Are you doing that God has told you to do? He will use it to fulfill His promises. Trust Him.

Chapter 6

Covenant Brotherhood

There is nothing better than a friend in the midst of turmoil. Many men can relate to that truth. It is not uncommon for men to cultivate friendships. The success of gangs and fraternities is evidence that the community of brotherhood offers an opportunity for bonding and accountability. These communities provide men a sense of family, mission, acceptance, and identity. These things are pivotal to the overall success of a brotherhood.

Some brotherhoods develop out of convenience. The friendship is not really based on anything substantial. For example, I had a few friendships in high school. During the final months of my senior year of high school, as the custom goes, I passed my yearbook around for people to sign. There were people who added their phone numbers and encouraged me to stay in touch. Unfortunately, I did not think we had a relationship worth building because our communication had been very limited.

Our "friendship" was emerged by default because we

attended the same school, took the same classes, ate lunch at the same table or even spent detention in the same hall. We were around each other so much that our connection and communication developed out of being in the same surroundings. Our communication led to common interests, but those interests were limited to school hours. I did not spend time with them after school. We did not hang out on weekends. Our friendship was built on convenience.

I have also had friendships that were alliances. It was not that we agreed on everything; it is that we agreed on a few foundational principles. Being conservative socially and politically, I have been able to connect with men who share those common principles. Our relationship was an alliance where we were able to align ourselves under one mission and stand against those who opposed us. This became very useful for me when I was deciding whether or not to run for political office. Those relationships represented an important alliance.

On the opposite end of the spectrum, I had friendships that were based on what I we stood against. For example, my high school was one of many under the threat of losing its accreditation because of the incompetent leadership of our school board members. As the class president and a student activist, I confronted the school board at a meeting. I saw some of my classmates there who I did not personally like because of childish reasons; nevertheless, we developed a relationship after I addressed the school board because we found a common ground in being in opposition to the school board's incompetence. I looked beyond the things I did not like and we became "strange bedfellows" to our mutual benefit.

There are also people who are seasonal friends. They enter your life for a particular time. In fact, these friends develop at a pivotal time in your life. Any number of circumstances—the death of loved one, a move to a new town, the start of a new job—and suddenly you become fast friends. These relationships are not planned. They simply happened at the right time; for the right purpose; with the right people. Just like seasons, these friendships change. Don't be alarmed when these friends change. Just as the seasons change, so may these friendships. In fact, new growth occurs when something is dying and has to be pruned.

I believe true friends, who ultimately become brothers, are able to stand the test of time. They are able to grow into covenant relationship because their friendship does not have to be convenient. These are the friends who with you through thick and then. The geographical distance between you is never an issue. You're usually just a phone call, a drive, or an airplane flight away from each other.

They do not need a reason to visit your home. They go in your fridge and sit in your favorite chair. These are people who are more than friends. Blood could not make them any closer. They share a special bond that only God can create. It is sealed with a mutual understanding of respect, honor, and love. This is a covenant brotherhood.

I have had many friendships throughout my life, but I have only encountered a few covenant brothers. Although I know many men, I know very few covenant brothers. They are men I can call at any time to talk about any thing. They hold me accountable and make sure I am always focused on what is pure and holy. They constantly point me back to Christ and keep my eyes fixed on eternity, not the temporary. We can laugh, cry, and ultimately grow together. These men are not perfect, but they aspire daily to be proficient in all they do. Covenant brothers understand the tricks of the enemy to divide and conquer.

With a discerning spirit, covenant brother arrest the plans of the enemy and render him ineffective. They have each other's backs and warn of desires or temptations that are dangerous.

It is not uncommon to see a group of men with their backs to the wall as they watch women walk past them. They have a strong desire to gain the attention of a woman they desire. Not all desires are bad. What needs to be considered is the object of one's desire.

What has become desirable to you? Notice in Genesis where Eve was talking to the serpent. The serpent convinced her that she would not die if she ate from the tree of the knowledge of good and evil. Eve did not eat from it until she noticed the fruit was desirable. Her perception of the fruit that God told Adam not to eat changed. Instead of staying away from it, she desired it as food to make her wise. Do you see the danger in some desires?

Covenant brothers know the enemy's desire is to have his way with them. These brothers know the devil wants to have them for his purpose. He wants you to do his bidding. He desires for you to do his work. Like the man standing on the corner, he is watching you. He craves your attention and will stop at nothing to change your perception about what God has commanded you not to do. He wants you to get to a point where you look at His commands and think to yourself, "I will not die." He wants you to think delayed punishment means consequences may not necessarily come. The enemy wants you to yield to lustful desires that will cause you to want more of the world and less of God. This is why your covenant brothers are so important to the growth and health of your faith.

I highly recommend that you do not stray far from your covenant brothers. If you do not have any, I encourage you to pray and ask God to send some into your life. That was my prayer for years. I grew up with one sibling, an older sister. I always desired an older brother. I wanted someone to teach me, hold me accountable, someone I could talk to, someone I could socialize with, someone I could wrestle with, and someone I could look up to. I did not get the blood brother I wanted. But, do you know God is faithful to prayer? He answered my prayer with covenant brothers who understand the weight I bear in ministry.

They understand what I mean when I say, "I am tired!" They hold me up when I am weak. They build me up when I am falling apart. These men will not hold anything back from me. They have seen me at my best and at my worst and still loved me through it. These are covenant brothers—men with a God-like heart and God-like passion. Their desire is to see me kneel before Christ and receive my rewards like a good and faithful servant. That is my desire for them also.

Do you have these kind of brothers in your life? If not, I want you to pray for them. Ask God to reveal those men to you who need to be in your life. Do not be afraid to reach out to them and establish a covenant brotherhood. Do not be afraid to let your guard down and let them see what is going on in your heart. Let them see the real you. Be willing to be held accountable.

If you are a wife, I encourage you to support your husband's godly friendships. Pray that God will send men of integrity into his life that can grow into strong friendships. He needs someone he can talk to other than you. Everything he says or wants to say cannot always be comprehended by you. Let him go and talk to his covenant brother about it. Allow them to encourage and redirect him to the truth. The key is not to push him into friendships but to encourage him to discover the friends God has just for him.

In the beginning of our marriage, my wife would ask me to go to dinner with other married couples. I would protest the entire time. I knew what she was trying to do. She wanted me to befriend the husband. I knew it was a setup. During these dinners, I would sit there and listen as these guys would go on and on talking about their accomplishments and other things they were trying to do. Knowing that I am a pastor, some guys would quote scripture as if they were trying to impress me with their knowledge of the Bible. I'm not opposed to discussing the Bible at diner, but sometimes I simply wanted to eat a nice meal and share small talk.

At some point, I would give my wife our signal to say, "Let's wrap this up." It never fails that men who are too verbose are either uncomfortable or trying to cover a deficiency in some other area. I would always ask myself, what is this man trying to hide? Because of the gift of discernment God has given me, it's difficult to sit down and just listen to someone talk. I begin to analyze every word through the filter of the Holy Spirit. Ultimately, I encourage women to be patient with a man's development of friends. Just know that many men are different from women in that department.

I have been in the company of men who truly treasure the bond of friendship. They are willing to give everything they have to the relationship. What they desire is to be surrounded by men who are committed to maturity, righteous fun, and accountability. They want to grow with their friends—iron sharpening iron—neither one has to stop or slow down to catch up with the other. All of the men I know who feel as I do about covenant brothers are men who grew up without brothers. Many of them are only children or some have only female siblings. Others grew up without a father in the household. No matter the situation each one of them desires brothers they can talk to, confide in, be honest with, and not feel condemned by.

Wives, do not undermine your husband's desire to have friends—specifically, male friends. It is not an option for me as a married man to have female friends. There is absolutely nothing I need to talk about with another woman. The only woman I care to talk to is my wife. I will talk to my mother and my sister, but my wife is the only woman who I communicate with. That is not something my wife mandated in our marriage; it is something I practice to allow for my wife to feel secure in knowing that I said "no" to every other woman when I said "yes" to her. The same is true for my wife. She does not have male friends. Those are boundaries we do not cross.

My wife and I have a practice that I encourage you and your spouse to adopt. It works well in our household. My wife goes on an annual women-only trip each year with her friends and I go on an annual men-only trip with mine. We travel to different cities around the globe with the intention of enjoying our friendship, confessing our sins to one another, praying for one another, and enjoying one another's company. It is always a good time. This trip gives both my wife and me the opportunity to retreat, refresh, and return home energized to continue in God's will.

Friendships are important. Do not neglect them.

Chapter 7

No One Understands Me

After seven years of marriage, his infidelity with another woman came to light. His wife was infuriated. The other woman did not want to leave him alone. Instead, she connected with his wife through social media to tell her about their short-lived affair, which included sexual encounters. For him, it was merely sexual; for her, it was the beginning of something beautiful. For his wife, it was severe damage to their marriage, a slap in her face, a shot through her heart, destruction to the unity of their engagement, and the end of their relationship.

The wife was a hurt and angry woman because of the actions of her husband. The husband was angry and hurt at the actions of the other woman. The other woman was pleased to see the marriage falling apart. She thought she could replace the wife. She was willing to settle for another woman's husband instead of believing God for her own—without thinking that someone who cheats once has the propensity to cheat again.

After sitting down with the husband, I inquired about his

reasoning for infidelity. I wanted to know why he did it. I needed answers, but I needed the answers from him. His wife had many different ideas and reasons as to why she thought he would do it, but those reasons were not validated. I needed to hear it from the source.

The husband looked at me and said, "Cornelius, no one understands."

I have learned over the years that it is difficult to convince someone you do understand. It is best to allow them to arrive at the revelation that you are willing to listen to understand instead of hearing to condemn. I explained my desire to understand this man's reasoning, but it was impossible to fully understand why he refused to be open. I asked for the opportunity to hear what was going on in his head. After he thought about it for a moment, he turned to me and began to speak.

He grew up in a two-parent household where he saw his father and mother living together. However, he did not see them really engaging one another, physically, emotionally, or otherwise. He saw his father work hard to make money and his mother take care of things at home. He grew up in what is now known as a traditional Southern household where men and women practice traditional family roles—the man works and provides; the wife stays at home and raises the children.

His father never gave him "the talk" about women. All he knew was his body was changing and he strongly desired to practice all the things he saw in the pornographic movies he watched in secret. He started his sexual journey very early. He soon got tired of watching the actions of others. He no longer wanted to live in their fantasy world. He set out in search for women—not just one woman. His focus was not to engage and invest in one relationship for the rest of his life. He wanted to explore multiple relationships. Marriage would mean he was settling for one. That was not his reality. He was intentionally promiscuous and did not want to be saddled with being faithful to just one woman.

Although his father was present in the home, he was silent. He didn't hear his father talk about fidelity in marriage. It was not being taught; therefore, he was not in a hurry to learn it. He was ready to explore the field. His competitive nature added fuel to the fire. The testosterone running through his body was creating a desire to cultivate and subdue—the very actions God gave to Adam to fulfill. The surge of testosterone was like liquid crack flowing through his veins. He wanted to run, jump, play, climb, and compete!

He found his outlet in American football. He loved playing the game and he played it well. He was religious about being in the weight room building muscle to be even better at the sport. His desire for the game was simple; he wanted to win. Winning for him consisted of two main components: learning the plays and scoring points. His desire for women and the thrill of football became a dangerous combination for him. Football taught him how to score. He began to use that same concept when it came to women.

God told Adam to subdue, which means "to conquer or to

take over." Man has a natural inclination to subdue, and it becomes dangerous when he does not have boundaries. Genesis 1:28 is where God commands His created beings to subdue the earth. However, God did not leave man without instruction. He gave Adam a command in Genesis 2:16-17, which was to make sure he did not eat from the tree of the knowledge of good and evil.

God told Adam that he could subdue the entire earth; he just had to leave that one tree alone. This is why it is good for man to be instructed about his boundaries and limitations. Left to his own devices, man might seek to act on his natural inclination to be fruitful, multiply, subdue, and rule, without any boundaries or limitations.

The game of football was quickly becoming this husband's his teacher for life. His focus was keeping score and learning the plays. It did not matter if the plays were illegal or not. He just wanted to make sure he scored. And sex meant that he scored. But the game needed to be left on the football field! You cannot celebrate a touchdown too long. You have to focus on the next one. Man will use these distorted rules in his dealings with women. He wouldn't want to be emotionally strapped to one woman. In his rulebook, the relationship had to be completely physical. What some men ignore is that intercourse involves a person's mind, spirit, and body.

It is not uncommon for a woman to desire the man who is perceived as the alpha male of the pack. It's common to see the quarterback or the biggest linebacker swarmed by women. They do not want the field goal kicker. They want the alpha male, the top dog, the crème-de-la-crème. As a star player on the team, this man had no shortage of women. Settling down with one of them was not a part of his plan. He just wanted to act out his own lustful desires with the women who were throwing themselves at him. His problem was not women; his problem was being educated on the rules.

Rules and regulations help govern our lives so that things run in decency and in order. God is orderly. He has rules that govern His church and the universe. No man is capable of usurping God's authority. When those rules are broken, there have to be consequences. Thankfully, Grace appeared in the flesh to offer all men the opportunity to escape the wrath that is reserved for those who break those rules. Jesus Christ is that Grace, and He exhorts men to resist sin, not stay in it. He simplifies the rules and makes our union with Him about relationship. Although we have a relationship with Him, we cannot afford to forget about the rules.

Our salvation is granted by faith, and our actions show that our faith has life. Rules cannot save. However, the concept of boundaries in our lives is righteous. We are thankful that our relationship—with the indwelling power of the Holy Spirit—convicts and pleads the cause for holiness. He guides us to know what to do and what not to do. Our relationship with Him is valuable. Relationship without rules brings chaos. Relationship with rules brings order and restraint. A righteous man who is compelled by the power of the Holy Spirit understands the concept of relationship and he is restrained by the rules of that relationship. In fact, the Holy Spirit develops within us the fruit of self-control. He restricts us, which ultimately supports the health of our relationship with Him.

The Bible encourages fathers to teach their children. We are to raise up our children in the truth and fear of the Lord. This does not mean a father teaches his children a bunch of rules; it means he teaches them about the importance of being in relationship with Christ through belief and confession. He teaches the importance of faith. He teaches the purpose of the relationship so his children can fully understand the purpose of the rules. Again, rules without relationship create chaos. Fear is the motivation of this practice. Rules with relationship create order. Respect is the primary motivation of this practice.

The man I used as an illustration, who played football and women, used the rules he learned in football to govern his life and lead his decision-making process. Women became a way for him to score in the game of life. The more women he had, the greater the score he could rack up. In talking with him, I could tell he had a high score, but he quickly learned that his score meant nothing if he did not follow God's righteous order. God's purpose for relationship between a man and a woman existed within the boundaries of marriage, not continuous in sexual immorality.

This man went through his life picking and choosing rules he wanted to follow. He said he did not have anyone in his life to properly guide him in a way that was righteous in the eyes of God. He, like many men, thought marriage would somehow reduce his desire to score with women. He quickly learned it could not. He had to understand that a lion does not stop being a lion just because he is put in a different cage. The lion has an innate desire to hunt and scavenge. He still desires to fight and protect his domain. The lion still desires to be in charge. The bars contain his body, but his mind is still wired for the hunt, the chase, and the capture.

The challenge arises in marriage when a man's body may be contained in one home and in the marriage bed with his wife, but his mind is still wired to subdue and to rule. If he has not confessed Jesus as Lord and Savior and been filled with the Holy Spirit, then he may have a tendency to subdue and rule outside of his home, disgracing his family and rebelling against God in the process. A truly honorable man should be concerned with keeping one woman pleased for the rest of their days together.

I sat down with a frustrated young man a few years ago. He spent most of his teenage years chasing fast money and loose women. He sold illegal substances every chance he could get, and he constantly had a different woman on his arm. He found pride in what he could acquire. There was one major problem—he had not developed the proper character to retain what he was catching. It did not matter how he obtained the money. His concern was not getting caught.

Godly character would have convicted him to seek legal employment or entrepreneurship to properly retain all he worked hard to attain. Instead, his constant striving for the next quick fix resulted in him feeling dissatisfied and empty. He told me how he made thousands upon thousands of dollars, but he kept none of it. He, like many men, was able to catch a lot, but the true test of manhood is found in how a man is able to retain what he has "caught."

I have met men who brag about the number of women they have been with sexually, but none of them were married. They took a righteous command to subdue and perverted it. They took a righteous command and began to use it unrighteously. One of the married men I mentioned earlier told me that he wanted to be released from the prison of his marriage. He said to me, "Cornelius, I love my wife, but I found myself practicing something I thought was right." Some people may roll their eyes when they read that and say he was just giving another excuse. And those who do are right to an extent. However, the husband was trying to operate in a righteous relationship, but he did not understand the rules of it. It is like trying to play basketball using the rules of football. He cannot show up on the court to play basketball fully suited for football. Each game has its own set of rules. A man must know the rules of the game if he truly desires to be successful.

For this man, it was about having and maintaining a high score. Unfortunately, his method of scoring included breaking many women's hearts and almost ending his marriage. He was risking the loss of his family to maintain a high score. This is no different than what he practiced in the game of football. Each time he got on the field he was willing to put his body on the line to score one more time. He was living by this idea: He who scores the most points wins the game. His being with multiple women was just another point to help his ultimate score in the game of life.

After locating his mindset I began to go before the Lord in prayer on his behalf. He recognizes the error of this ways now. In fact, he knew his ways were wrong when he was contacting other women while he was married. Although he knew the "rules" of commitment and trust in a marriage, he did not understand why he needed to actually practice them. He had rules without relationship, and there was no fear there to make sure he followed them.

I am proud to report that he has confessed Jesus as Lord and Savior. He is also filled with the Holy Spirit. He has a solid relationship with God now. His actions have changed because his mindset has changed. The way he lived before was a direct result of the way he thought. He lives differently now because his mind has been renewed. Romans 12:2 reads "*And do not be conformed to this world, but be transformed by he renewing of your mind, so that you may prove what the will of God is, that which is good and acceptable and perfect.*" This husband knew of God before, but his mind was not renewed to yield to the ways of God. Now, his mind has been renewed, his life is changed, and his marriage is stronger than ever.

I have been asked countless times why men cheat as if only men cheat. Women cheat, too. It is not about gender as much as it is about their mindset in connection with the Christian lifestyle. A woman or man who is not in relationship with the Holy Spirit through Jesus Christ is not capable of truly understanding righteous principles. They are foolishness and nonsense to the unsaved man or woman. Giving them rules is like placing a wild lion in a cage.

I've known married couples who put on a public show of love for one another. In one case, after more than a dozen years of pretending, a man presented his wife with divorce papers. They ended up in my office. The wife was completely baffled about what happened.

She explained through her tears, "We just celebrated our anniversary. He took me to our favorite restaurant. He bought me my favorite flowers. We stayed at our favorite hotel. He made sure everything was perfect. I just do not understand." Her husband just sat there emotionless. He looked straight ahead. His wife thought his attentiveness was genuine. Actually his special treatment was merely learned responses that he perfected over the years. He was like a wild lion who had been taught to leap, jump through hoops, and roar on command. His actions were mastered, but his heart was unchanged. Like any wild animal, this husband escaped from his "cage" when the opportunity presented itself.

I know what it is like to be misunderstood. After speaking with the husband, I understood one important thing about him. It was not just that he felt like no one understood him; he did not really understand himself. You can see why it is vital to be quickened with new life through Jesus and truly filled with the Holy Spirit. He will restrain you, teach you, comfort you and guide you.

Chapter 8

Unwanted

I have a newfound understanding of my father's silence.

After a very intense disagreement with my wife, my son looked at me and said, "No, Papa!" Was it an innocent blurt? Possibly. However, it was a stab in the heart for me. I felt like my son chose sides. He picked his favorite. He chose his mother over me.

Do I believe my wife and I have to fight over the attention and affection of our child? No. But becoming a father has really made me think about many things concerning my life and my children. It has also caused me to reexamine my childhood and my relationship with my father.

The look on my son's face as he clung tightly to my wife broke my heart. I have heard countless times how sons love and adore their mothers. I know this personally because of my fondness for my mother. I called her for everything. If I did not think I needed her, I tried to do whatever I thought needed to be done on my own. If I was desperate, I would call my father. He was my last resort. That is not the case for some men I know. They have great relationships with their father, and I admit I have envied that kind of relationship. I wanted my father to love me, talk to me, affirm me, lead me, and correct me. I vowed never to be like my father.

My son was only two-years-old at the time of this particular incident. As a toddler, there was no preference. As a nursing baby, I understood he knew where his nourishment came from and that established a uniquely bonded relationship.

My wife and I share certain responsibilities with our son, but some were specific to my wife. She is a terrific mother who can begin her day, up before sunrise, cradling our son in her arms or getting him an early morning juice or water. Their bond is undeniable but my grief was not directed at my wife's maternal ability to care and provide for our son. It was about my son seeming to choose my wife over me. That bothered me deeply.

I started to think about all the times he ran to her when he was hurt. He would walk right past me and ask her to do something for him. I could be in the same room with him, but he would go to another part of the house, yell for my wife, and ask her to do something that I could have done. I started to think about the times he cried and whined when she was around because he knew he would get his way.

All I could imagine was my son pushing me out of his life and indirectly excluding me as source of comfort or provision. That one moment cut so deeply, I got in my car and went for a drive alone around the city of Atlanta for about an hour. It was a little past midnight. I had enough time to drive and think. And this led me to grow more and more empathic and understanding of my father.

I began to ask myself if I was responsible for shutting him out of my life. I know I cannot take total responsibility for my father's silence, but this incident allowed me to see that I was partly at fault for the distance in our relationship. I know I did not tell him I didn't want him around, but I believe my actions suggested that I had excluded him from my life on some level.

I criticized him for not being present at my high school activities. He was absent from the award nights. He only came to one of my junior high football games. He never showed up at any of my sports camps. He was not there when I gave my first speech as president of my high school student council. He was absent and silent for many big moments in my life.

After thinking about it, I came to a very profound conclusion: I never invited him! I never called him and told him about the award nights. I never told him about the speeches I would give. I never told him about my games. I assumed he should know because he was my father. I assumed he should have known because I told my mother. I would ask her to pass the information on to him. That is completely disrespectful. I did not think enough of him to talk to him face to face. Instead, I would speak to him through my mother. Suddenly I could understand my father's pain and silence.

While sitting in my car after that drive around the city, I wondered if my father felt the same way. I wondered if he felt like he did not need to do anything or go anywhere because I had not invited him. No one wants to feel unwanted or left out. We all want to feel needed and accepted. That feeling of being left out or disengaged is a difficult pill to swallow.

My son's response to me that night was evidence. I wanted him to call on me like he called on his mother. I wanted him to climb on me and hug me. My wife is the symbol of nurture and care. I am his symbol for wrestling. I am his human punching bag. He hugs his mother and punches me. He walks up to my wife and says, "Mom, your hair is pretty." Then he turns around to me and says, "No, papa!" and kicks me in the shin.

When I returned home after driving around the city, I walked back in the house with tears in my eyes. My heart was broken, and I felt like I could truly understand my father a little better. I could no longer place blame on him. It is highly possible that he was very silent and absent because I was never inviting or warm towards him. I preferred my mother over him, and I made sure he knew that daily. I am sure that broke his heart.

I also wanted to have a son to bond with as a true father and son team. I can only imagine how disheartening it would be for a father to see his son prefer someone over him—especially another man. And I know I did this countless times in front of my father. I sought dynamic, encouraging mentors because my father was not expressive or nurturing. But I probably never knew that I wanted him to be involved in my life. I never invited him. I just assumed he would be because he was my father.

If you are a mother, I caution you not to have a smothering

type of relationship with your son. Do not give him the grounds to play sides. Encourage him to talk, confide in, and love on his father. Because we fathers need it! I know I need it. I want to be affirmed as a father. I want my child to respond to me. If you are a mother, encourage your children to be expressive in their love, affection, and respect for their father. Above all do not be critical of your husband. Refrain from any negative words about your son's father. Discourage any sign of favoritism between parents. I have met some men who were not the best husbands, but they were fantastic fathers. The roles can intersect, but they are not the same. Do not separate them. Sons need fathers. Although sons may have a special affection for their mothers, they mature in the discipline and guidance of their fathers.

It could very well be that the man in your life is silent because he feels unwelcome. He could feel that he does not have an invitation in the lives of his children. He could also feel that he is not welcome in your world either. It could be that you have your set of friends, your job, your money, your things, and your ideas that you never share with him. He does not feel welcome at all. He feels like a guest in an area that is supposed to be a shared world. He has so much to say, but he says nothing.

If this is your husband and the father or stepfather of your children, be cautious of putting your children before him. Show your man that you love and respect him. Tell him that he is more than enough. Reassure him that he is doing the best he can with what he has been given. And if you feel that he does not deserve any praise whatsoever, I ask that you think of some things he does right and encourage him with those things. If all he does is put his socks in the right drawer, then cheer him on each time he does it. Be prayerful about all the things you think he needs to improve instead of nagging him. He already has the world against him; he does not need an enemy in his own house. Nagging has never changed a man. Only God has the power to change him.

If you are reading this to understand your silent and absent father, I encourage you forgive him of the past. Empathize with him by looking at things from his perspective. You could have very well invited him to all of your school activities, but he chose not to show up. He could have prioritized everything and everyone over you. Forgive him, pray for him, and ask God to show you ways to communicate and love him back to life. He could feel abandoned. Those who hurt others are usually hurt themselves. Do not let him go to his grave feeling like he was all alone and misunderstood.

If you are a man looking to grow, I encourage you to learn how to communicate what is in your heart. I understand people do not know everything about you. They do not understand the existence of pain in your life. They do not understand your feelings of inadequacy and abandonment, but do not make them pay for the hurt in your heart.

Love the people around you enough to communicate with them. You are wanted and you are needed. You are special. You are more than enough. God has a purpose for you. He has not abandoned you. Your future does not have look like your past. How you finish does not have to look the way you started. Get up and encourage yourself in the Lord. I believe in you, brother. I am cheering you on to endure this race we call life. With Christ, you can do it!

Chapter 9

Struggling for Survival

I have written a great deal about my struggle with pornography and sex, but I want to devote this chapter to exposing the truth of what it means to struggle and fight. Truthfully, what I called struggling with sin was not struggling at all; it was more of me constantly giving in to it. I gave in to the temptations at every opportunity. I would think about watching pornography as I sat in the front row of church.

Sex was not my only issue. I also had a major issue with overeating. I hated the way I looked, so I found comfort in food. I ate and ate and ate. I was a gluttonous mess. My physical trainer would ask me how I was doing, and I would tell lie after lie. I did not want to admit that I loved the affirmation I got from food more than I loved the discipline and results I knew I could get from working out and eating a healthy diet.

After going to the gym regularly for a reasonable period of time, my trainer looked at me and said, "You are not losing any weight. There is no change at all! What's going on?" I knew I could not lie any longer. The scale told the truth that my lies could not cover. I finally came clean and told him everything. He said to me, "Cornelius, there is no way I can possibly help you if you are not willing to help yourself!" Those words were so true. I realized I was my worst enemy. I was fighting progress instead of fighting the very thing that was holding me back. I could no longer claim that I was struggling; I was giving in. I was fully giving in.

I had a buddy of mine who lived alone for many years. His apartment was in a high crime area. There had been a large number of break-ins, and he was taking the necessary precautions to make sure he and his belongings were safe. His apartment was on the third floor, so he did not think he would be an easy target. But the fact is a thief was watching his every move and was studying his habits. He knew when he left, what roads he took to work and what time he returned from work.

On the day the thief was prepared to make his move and break-in to the apartment, my buddy received a call from his boss telling him that he would work from home. The thief watched as the man he thought was my buddy get in the car and he left around the exact same time my buddy left for work. The thief got out of his car, walked up the flight of stairs to the apartment.

Inside, my buddy was preparing a cup of coffee and some breakfast. The kitchen was not too far away from the door. While standing in the kitchen, my buddy heard what sounded like the doorknob rattling. He walked into the living room to see that it looked and sounded like someone was trying to break-in to his residence. He got himself ready, called the police and prepared for a battle. The door swung open and my buddy immediately grabbed the thief. A full-blown battle began. They fought one another from the doorway to the kitchen. Neither one of them wanted to give up, but my buddy soon got the upper hand. All those years of endurance training came in handy. The would-be thief finally surrendered. My buddy held him down until the police arrived.

That story also made me think about 'struggling bouts' in the past. My buddy knew the thief was coming. Instead of going to hide, he stood and prepared to fight. He also made sure he called for backup. He did not go into the struggle alone.

I used my buddy's example to teach me about my need to fight against those things I knew God hates like sexual immorality, lying, cheating, anger, and anything else He hates. Unlike my buddy, I was not fighting back; I was giving in. I was not calling for help. I did not go into prayer when temptation was at its peak. I was not calling on my accountability partners when I was at my weakest. I was giving in, and I was doing it often.

My buddy told me that it was either him or the thief. He felt like it was life or death. He was fighting for his life. I had to adopt that same mindset when I was wrestling with sexual temptation. I had to recognize the danger of it. I could not allow it to continue to ruin me. Every click at the computer; every DVD; every late night sexual encounter was me giving in—again. It was as if I died each time. I had to refuse to die seeing that Christ already died for my freedom.

I have heard many stories similar to the attempted theft

in my friend's home. Some stories did not end like his. Some people were overcome by thieves and killed. You must adopt the honorable death idea when it comes to overcoming temptation. You must be willing to battle against it even unto death. You can have self-control against temptation. The Holy Spirit produces the fruit within us. Yield yourself to Him. I remember the words of my trainer. As he said, there was no way he could help me if I was not willing to help myself.

Those who are filled with the Holy Spirit have the ability to resist temptation. He convicts us and pleads the case for holiness. He leads us out of temptation. Help Him help you by yielding to His power and taking that way of escape when temptation comes. When He convicts you not to do something, obey Him immediately. He will always teach and lead you in the way of our Lord Jesus.

I do not know if you are currently struggling for survival right now. If you are, I encourage you to continue the fight. Do not let it go. This is for your survival! Your life is on the line. Your character is on the line. Your integrity is on the line. Everything you have worked hard to attain is on the line. Do you really want to lose it all because of temporary pleasure.

I encourage you to rise and fight! Temptation is standing outside the door. The knob is turning. What will you do? Will you fight? Will you rise and battle with everything within you? Or will you give in, lie down, and allow it to have its way over you? Never forget that he who struggles is actively engaged in the fight.

Giving in means you have no more fight left in you. Fight, brother! Fight!

Chapter 10

Not Good to be Alone

"Then the Lord God say, "*It is not good for the man to be alone; I will make him a helper suitable for him.*" (Genesis 2:18)

These words are potent—filled with truth and bursting at the seams with life. It is a wonderful thing for the Creator to notice that His creation does not need to be alone. Man has been gifted with the responsibility to cultivate, subdue, be fruitful, multiply, fill the earth, and have dominion. His physical body is made to carry a heavy load. His mind is made to think beyond the ordinary to fulfill the tasks he is given.

In Genesis 1:31, we notice that everything God created was good. Until, that is, He notices that Adam is alone. This was not a good thing. God did not leave this situation incomplete. He finished what He started. He needed to fix it, and His solution was to create Eve.

Man cannot be left alone. He cannot be left to his desires; his way of thinking; his ambitions. I have heard it said that a world without women would be a world filled with war and rage.

Countries would battle one another as a sport. While I believe there would be some commonsense approaches to the way we govern overselves, we would live like untamed beasts. The idea or thought of sensitivity would probably be out of the window. I know how much my life changed after I was married to Heather. I started living alone when I was nineteen-years-old. I did not want a roommate partly because I wanted to be alone. I started out in a three-bedroom townhouse before finally moving into a four-bedroom two-story home. It was much more than I needed, and honestly, much more than what I could afford. However, I wanted the space.

I did not decorate at all. My living room, which was large enough to entertain a large party, was empty. I had no pictures on the walls. My kitchen was bare. I had a glass table that was gifted to me. I still had the plastic over the cushions because I did not want them to get dirty. I had a few dishes and mostly ate on plastic ware and drank out of bottles. There were no curtains at my windows. I used the same blinds to cover the windows that were left in the house when I purchased it.

I needed a woman's touch to brighten up my house and turn it into a home. After we were married, Heather did just that. She transformed the entire place. I had scented candles burning nightly after I was married. She painted walls, hung pictures, and so much more. She gave my home a womanly touch that I was much more than I could imagine. Am I saying men cannot decorate? Absolutely not. However, I believe there is a touch only a woman can give to bring balance and a sense of elegance. God's decision to create the woman is a stroke of creative genius.

While sitting in a men's ministry meeting one Saturday, a young man started telling me about some things going on with him. He had recently moved down to Atlanta to attend our church. Over the years, we have had many people to take that leap of faith. It did not hurt that he found his wife in Atlanta as well. He believed he was doing exactly what God told him to do. However, he told me about a strong uneasiness he kept experiencing. He wanted to sleep all day long. If he was not sleeping, he was eating. He was trying to find some way to fill the voids in his heart. He could not explain his own behavior.

I could empathize with him because I have felt those same emotions in the past. After my wife and I moved to Mississippi, I began to experience the same symptoms. All I wanted to do was eat and sleep. It was a fight just to get out of bed. I wanted to argue with my wife over the smallest things. It was incredibly rough and a tough time for me. I wanted to give up on life. The young man felt the same way.

After listening to his dilemma, I said to him, "Brother, it is possible for you to be in the right house but be in the wrong room." This is what I mean. He knew he was supposed to be in Atlanta, Georgia. He knew his move was the right decision. He knew he was at the right church. He felt his overall position was right where it needed to be. Unfortunately, he was devoting his time and energy to something other than what he knew he was supposed to be doing.

He is a preacher. A guy once asked me how he could

confirm his call to be a preacher. I said to him, "If you wake up preaching, go throughout your day preaching, preach to empty seats, preach to your dog, preach to your cat, and preach going to bed, you are a preacher." Preaching is not my profession; it is my passion.

Although the young man was in the right place, he was not doing the right thing. He was in the right house, but he was in the wrong room. I encouraged him to start preaching again. It did not matter where he preached. The important thing was for him to begin to preach. He took my advice, and those symptoms of depression went away. The action of doing something worthy took away the idea that he was worth nothing and doing nothing. It was a powerful testimony.

The young man's depressive state was leading him to be alone, and we know it is not good for man to be alone. In fact, it is not good for anyone to be alone. We are made in God's image and likeness. God is a relational being; therefore, we are relational beings. We need relationships. Many men feel alone because they build walls to keep people out instead of building bridges to lasting friendships.

The idea of being alone is not a good one. Being alone makes a man become more selfish and more independent. God calls men to be selfless, not selfish. Relationship requires selflessness not selfishness. God also calls us to be interdependent, not independent. Being interdependent means we depend on one another.

Independence means one is free from the dependence on

another person. Our faith is about dependence. We are dependent on Christ and we share that same dependence with our brothers in accountability, spiritual growth, and teaching. It does not matter how anyone tries to glorify being alone; it is never a good thing.

Do not run to be alone. Aloneness brings alienation. You cannot hide from God. I encourage you to remove the fig leaves you are using to hide behind. It is time to burn down walls you have built and start building bridges.

Chapter 11

The Angry Man

As I sat down to lunch with Sam, a family man with a wife and three beautiful children, the cast on his hand immediately caught my attention. .

Why the cast? Sam became so enraged over something his wife said to him that he hit a wall with his fist, which resulted in three broken fingers. He told me he was ashamed to tell anyone what really happened so he explained the bandaged hand as a mixed martial arts accident.

Always well-dressed and a well-respected man in the community, Sam won many awards for community service. Several non-profits named him to their board because of his generous donations. He was a wealthy man who was able to provide anything and everything his family desired. His wife did not have to work outside of the home and his children were already preparing for college, which Sam would easily finance.

It seemed Sam and his family had it all. However, his uncontrollable anger was Sam's hidden flaw. This was not the first time he put holes in the wall or caused major damage to his personal belongings or to the people he said he loved. Not only did his violent temper result in physical harm to people or things but he had gone to the extreme of setting things on fire. His family did all they could not to upset him.

His anger began as verbal abuse. It soon graduated to physical abuse. The children were beaten and shaken by him whenever they were disobedient or disorderly. If he felt they did anything out of order, or any behavior disrupted his militaristic-style of order, their punishment was severe. One of the most extreme encounters he had was with his son. Sam broke his son's arm in a fit of rage when he discovered that the boy's room was not clean. His wife suffered black eyes and bruises on her body at Sam's hand. No one in the community knew about Sam's anger. It was a secret kept behind the closed doors of his home.

His rage was intense and furious and it increased when he drank alcohol. Often the anger seemed to come out of nowhere. The smallest things could set him off. He was a walking time bomb. Most times, his anger would silence his family and cause them to quickly do whatever he demanded of them. They could tell when the anger was coming on because it was usually preceded by an intense stare intended to intimate his victims into submission. He would frequently give them the silent treatment and make them think they were responsible for his actions.

Sam caused enough confusion to make his family actually believe they were the cause for his anger. He was a skilled manipulator who played the victim in most scenarios. He did this to gain sympathy for his erratic behavior. His family would take the bait over and over again. They would console him to assure him of their love in hopes that the verbal and physical abuse would stop.

I was proud of his decision to finally discuss the problem. After seeing professional counselors, which I recommended for him, Sam and I sat down to talk about his life. That conversation was intense and revealing. I know that angry man because I, too, was one of them.

We respond in anger to different situations because of irritation, frustration, displeasure, or pain. There was a time when I would get very angry on the highway if someone followed me too closely. I got so angry that I would drive as slowly as possible to irritate the person behind me. I have since learned how to manage that anger, but it did seem uncontrollable at one point. I would direct my anger towards the tailgating driver when really my anger had a completely different source.

Anger does not just affect the mind; it also affects the body. The autonomic nervous system increases the adrenaline in the body. Anger is one of the expressions of this process. Depending on the amount of adrenaline and noradrenaline in the body, we become aroused, excited, tense, or heated. Our blood pressure rises, our heart rate speeds up, and our digestive system fluctuates.

Unpleasant exchanges with people cause both physical and emotional responses. I can recall my experience of being chewed out by a boss because he felt I was at fault for his late arrival to an important meeting. As his assistant, I mapped out travel directions to and from an airport and he opted not to use the directions I provided. Instead, he took a different route because he felt the routes I identified would take too long. I was forced to sit before him and endure his tirade about being late for his meeting.

As I listened to his angry words, my face became flush; my heart rate sped up; my teeth were clinched; my stomach was churning; and my fists were clinched. I kept telling myself that I had to control my anger because not controlling it would cause me to lose my job. I knew the anger was coming on. I could feel it. I was about to make a conscious decision about whether or not I wanted to obey my feelings at that time. I had to weigh the pros and cons of the situation. I chose to sit and listen to him yell at me. Afterwards, I got up and went to my office. I was furious. I took a long walk to get away from the office and to calm down.

I have not always made good decisions like that when I became angry. There was one time when I became very angry over something my wife said to me. What she said reminded me of what others said in the past to make fun of me. While I know she was not intending to hurt me, I became angry—very anger! I became so enraged that I picked up a lamp and broke it on a nightstand. I was lucky that I did not cut my hand wide open. Nonetheless, I was very angry. I did not make the wisest choice. I chose an angry physical outburst.

There are two distinct manifestations of anger: the protector and the child. Every person has a protector and a child inside of him or her. The child is a sum total of the experiences one has from the time of birth. These experiences, whether good or bad, begin to greatly affect the way the child perceives life. For example, if a child has been repeatedly sexually abused by a close relative, the child begins to base his actions and perceptions of life through the lens of abuse. He becomes distant, angry, and unwilling to trust others. On the other hand, the life view of a child who experienced a healthier and harmonious home environment with a mother, father and siblings minus the dysfunction, would be influenced by that environment. Unlike the boy who was abused, this child would not necessarily have issues trusting others or isolating himself from others.

The protector in us is present to protect the child in us. The protector builds walls around the heart so people and circumstances cannot do harm to the vulnerable heart of the child. The protector responds to accusation or frustration with anger and a willingness to fight for the protection of the child—even with deadly force.

Childhood has such an impact on who a person becomes in adulthood. Ideally a child learns how to respond, not react. His emotions are communicated in a rational way. He silences the protector and handles the situations as they come. He knows that an inability to respond rationally will cause the protector to react. When the protector reacts, someone usually gets hurt.

For example, let's say the child inside of us experienced the pain of name-calling. As this child grows up, he still deals with the same pain even though he has yet to properly express his hurts. Although the inner child has the body and age of an adult, he still functions as a child within. If anyone chooses to call him anything that is remotely similar to the things he was called as a child, the protector will react. This reaction could be sarcasm, more name-calling, or physical violence. The protector literally erupts in an angry outburst. His goal is to protect the child from experiencing more hurt from the name-calling. Even when name-calling is in jest, the protector will react as if the tormentor has committed an act of war against the child.

Many times men react to protect our emotions and ego instead of responding soberly in the situation. Some do not respond outwardly. Some redirect their anger inwardly. They become depressed or choose to suppress their feelings. They try to bottle up their emotions in an attempt to make it seem like nothing is wrong. This process can lead to self-destructive behavior. This is where the person no longer has a good image of himself. He chooses to fill or deal with his suppressed anger by overeating, sleeping around, and other self-destructive behaviors. The angry man can either internalize his rage and destroy himself or allow for it to explode externally and hurt others.

Many times we grow angry because of unmet expectations. I met with a couple who was very upset with one another. The wife said, "Frank does not help me out with the children at all. He comes home from work and expects me to do everything. I cook. I clean. I make sure the bed is made. I make sure the children are taken care of. I make sure the house looks nice when he comes home. I do everything while he does nothing!"

When I look over at Frank, his face has turned red. He is about to explode. He lifted his head and said, "Cornelius, this woman never appreciates anything I do for her. She always complains! I took her out to dinner two nights ago. Did I get any appreciation at all? No! I cleaned the garage last weekend. She has not said a word. All I have asked her to do is show affection, and I cannot seem to get that from her. She is always so busy doing all these things she thinks I want and that I haven't asked for. I am sick of all of this!"

Notice that both Frank and his wife had expectations. She wanted him to help her with the kids; he wanted her to give him some affection. Although they were doing many things, they were not properly communicating to each other what they really desired. They were moving a million miles-per-hour, but they were not getting anywhere. In fact, their behavior was making matters worse. The wife, Lucy, explained that she was so exhausted from doing everything around the house that she didn't think about giving Frank any attention. Frank was doing everything Lucy said needed to be done so that he could receive the affection from her that he craved. They were both trying to do something for other without realizing what they wanted from the other. They never took the time to stop and talk about their expectations and desires, which would have made both very clear. Because Frank and Lucy were not meeting one another's expectations, they became frustrated. And their frustration led to anger. It almost ended their marriage.

They also did something else that I recommend you do not do. They used absolutes. These are words like "always," "never," and "every time." After I allowed Frank and Lucy to vent, I asked Lucy, "Has Frank taken time to help you with the children?" She said, "Yes. Of course." She chose to use an absolute—"never" and portrayed Frank inaccurately. She was angry, and she allowed her anger to get the best of her. I also asked her if she ever asked Frank if he wanted her to do the laundry list of chores that made her so exhausted. I wanted to know if Frank specifically said he desired for her to make the bed, cook the food, and all the other things she said. She looked at me and said, "No. I haven't asked him."

Lucy assumed Frank wanted those things done. Although they must be done, those were not specific things that Frank was requiring her to do. He was more than willing to pay someone to come in and help with the household chores and hire a babysitter from time to time to help with the children while he was at work. Lucy came to see that she was placing unreasonable expectations on herself. Frank was not requiring those things of her. Frank was asked the same question, and we came to the same conclusion. He was doing the same thing as his wife.

After another 45-minute conversation about their communication, they left with a new outlook on their marriage. They are one of the happiest couples I have seen in a long time. They were able to disarm their anger towards one another by addressing their expectations. I encourage you to do the same.

If you are married, sit down with your spouse and ask her

what she expects of you. I encourage you to be sober-minded as you listen to her. Notice I did not say you should respond. Just listen. After she is finished talking, discuss those expectations. Go through Scripture and see if God has given you those same expectations. If they do not align with the Word of God, then I do not encourage you do those things. For example, if she says she expects for you to buy her a new designer bag every week, I encourage you to ask her to adjust her expectation. Communicate what you can do and what you cannot do. The goal is to identify the frustrations so you can eliminate the anger.

If you are single, it is important that you identify your expectations now. You do not want to go into a relationship with unrealistic expectations. I encourage you to examine the expectations you have for yourself. Measure them by the Word of God to see if your expectations match His expectations. Then, make the proper adjustments. This is how you create a balanced view of self. This is important to curbing your anger.

If you are battling with anger issues, here are seven points that I hope will help you curb the anger.

1. Do not deny you are angry.

You have probably heard it said that 'admitting you are wrong is the first step to true healing.' There is so much truth in that statement. The same is true about anger. You must learn to admit you are angry and be able to verbalize it.

I did not realize how much anger I had bottled up in me

until I was married. It seemed my wife knew how to bring it out of me. In actuality, she was the closest person to me, and I became proficient in pushing people away if I felt they were getting too close to me. Since I was married I could not push her away. I had to do something I did not like to do—work it out civilly.

In the past I would use my words to hurt people. I had the ability to make people feel small. I started doing that to my wife and noticed I was doing it to myself. Marriage made us one, so whatever I did to her, I was doing to myself. I could not continue. We had several really destructive arguments. We said a lot of hurtful things to each other. Our aim was to injure one another as much as we could. We were succeeding. Things did not start improving in our marriage until we chose to recognize and discuss our expectations and admit to one another when we were angry.

Before words were thrown at one another we would say, "Baby, I am angry. Let's not discuss this right now." We then came up with a code word. Our code word is "Jesus." When we say "Jesus," all arguments cease. Neither person is allowed to say another word. That tells the other person that we are reaching a dangerous point of anger in our conversation. It does not mean we do not discuss what happened. It means we are willing to calm down and become sober-minded again. Then, we will discuss whatever it was we needed to talk about like mature adults. If we cannot reach an agreement, we will find a mediator—someone who is wise enough to hear both sides and come to a conclusion in line with the Word of God. My wife and I make it a practice to agree that we will take the mediator's wisdom before we seek him out. This practice has always worked for us.

Admitting you are angry is an act of humility. Do not feel you are weaker because you are wrong. It takes great strength to admit it. Be strong!

2. Do not feel guilty about your anger.

Ephesians 4:26 reads "*Be angry, and yet do not sin; do not let the sun go down on your anger.*"

Anger does not have to lead to sin. It is possible for someone to be righteously angry. As a believer it is appropriate for me to be angry over sin and hate all that God hates like pornography, incest, murder, racism, abuse of any kind, sex trafficking, etc. My righteous anger leads me to preach the Gospel and share the truth in hopes that the truth will stop any of these things from happening.

I am not condoning anger. I am only saying that you must not condemn yourself for being angry. I encourage you to find the root of your anger by analyzing your expectations.

3. Do not justify sin because you are angry.

Proverbs 12:16 reads "*A fool's anger is known at once, but a prudent man conceals dishonor.*" In other words, a fool is quick to act on his anger, but a wise man is able to overlook the insult. As you mature, it is important that you learn the value of not allowing the insults of others make you angry. You have to allow God to fight those battles for you. He will judge their wrongdoing and evil words. You just cannot allow your anger to elevate into sin.

I have been in many situations where I felt I could not control my anger; therefore, I justified my sin. In actuality I could control it; I just did not want to. I was blinded by rage, but I could feel it coming on. I am sure there are some medical cases where some have 'blacked out' due from such rage. I do know that those who are followers of Christ and are filled with the Holy Spirit have the ability to be angry, but the scripture exhorts us not to sin.

4. Do not let the day end without settling the anger in your heart.

Allowing anger to stay in your heart without addressing it is like packing bullets in a gun to use it for a future release. You will shoot those bullets. It is important to release them sooner than later, and the goal is to release them in a safe environment where others are not hurt.

Allowing anger to rest in your heart gives the enemy an opportunity to give more thoughts to grow the anger. He will convince you that you are doing the right thing by being angry and that your anger is justified. He will present the other person in such a way that you are convinced that it is okay for you to be upset with him or her. He will bring old situations to create new problems. He will lessen your part to play in the situation. The anger will incubate in your heart until you cannot contain it anymore. That is when you explode and act in an unrighteous way. Release the anger before you go to bed each night.

5. Be careful what you say.

Ephesians 4:31 reads "*Let all bitterness and wrath and anger and clamor and slander be put away from you, along with all malice.*"

When someone yells or raises his or her voice in an intimidating way, this is clamor. When a person's character is misrepresented with damaging speech and hateful words, this is slander. Malice is a type of wicked speech intended to injure a person. It does not build; it only tears down. These words usually provoke a violent reaction. Bitterness is expressed disappointment. It is also a type of resentment. Wrath is like anger on steroids.

As the verse urges us, we must put away all bitterness, wrath, anger, clamor, slander and malice. If not, those words will come out to injure others and damage our Christian witness.

6. Seek professional help

It is not always easy for men to ask for help, but I would highly recommend finding a Spirit-filled counselor who can help locate the root of your anger. I encourage you to seek professional help so you are healthy enough to lead and love your family. Seeking help does not make you weak; it is actually a show of great strength.

7. Learn how to communicate your thoughts without criticizing others.

You do not have to criticize others to get your point across. It is possible for you to communicate respectfully even when you are angry. If you feel like you are beginning to become critical, I urge you to confess that you are angry. Let the other person know that you need to take a break from the situation.

Do not make it a practice to talk about what the other person is doing to you. Instead, be willing to discuss what is going on with you. When you begin to discuss your part in the situation, anger can be disarmed. Reconciliation can come more quickly when people put down their guard. Just make sure you watch what you say. Words can cut as deeply as a knife. Please be careful what you say. Ultimately, you cannot silence your anger. You must confess it. You cannot heal what you do not confess.

I met a father of a beautiful little girl. Hank was an Information Technology professional with so much to offer in his field. He was a faithful husband to his wife. He did not have the best relationship with his mother during his childhood. Somehow the recollection of the anger towards his mother was turned towards his daughter. He spanked her frequently. His daughter crawled in his lap after he spanked her for spilling water on a carpet and said to him, "Your love hurts, Daddy." He could barely hold his head up when he said that to me. I could tell that it really hurt him.

He would tell his daughter that he had to spank her because he loved her. He had to realize that he was teaching his daughter to associate love with hurt and pain. This reality hit him so hard that it helped him make a change. He soon found a safe place to confess his past and to deal with the anger in his heart. He apologized to his daughter and has since developed a beautiful relationship with her. His daughter radiates with love, and I truly believe her father's change had a lot to do with it.

I encourage you to fix any relationships that have been destroyed because of anger. Ask for forgiveness where it is needed. Also be sure to forgive yourself. Do not allow anger to make you a silent, bitter man. Freedom is possible.

Chapter 12

I'm Lost

A man can be lost and no one around him will know it. He can deceive people into thinking he knows exactly where he is going. It will take an act of God for some men to open up their mouths to confess that they are lost.

After arriving in Kansas City, Missouri, my wife and I wanted to find our favorite grocery store chain. I did not want to use my phone to pull up directions. So I asked our rental car company to give me a map. Yes, they still make paper maps. I pulled over to the side of the road to map out where I needed to drive to reach our destination. After almost 30 minutes of driving, in what I thought was the right direction, we quickly discovered that we were going in the opposite direction. I realized that once we drove into a different state. My wife noticed the signs that were taking us away from our destination. I felt like we were lost, but I did not want to say anything. My pride and ego prevented me from opening my mouth and admitting that I was lost.

My wife and I have talked to many couples who find

themselves in the same scenario. Like me, the husband is driving and does not want to admit that he is lost. Why is it so difficult for men to admit when we're lost? It would seem fairly simple to admit it, right? Well, that is not always the case.

Many men do not know they are lost. We can look at this from a spiritual and an intellectual perspective. Spiritually, we know that the eyes of the blind are not opened until God opens them. Man does not have the capability of opening them himself. God, being sovereign, will have the final say on His will being done. However, God has provided man with the ability to make choices after his eyes are opened.

Jonah, best known for being in the belly of the whale, was told to deliver a message to Nineveh—the capital of Assyria. He did not want to do it since the Assyrians were a difficult people. God gave Jonah a directive, but still he disobeyed Him. After Jonah repented of his rebellion; he began his journey to Nineveh to deliver the prophecy. His obedience led to the Assyrians repenting of their actions.

Abraham, a major figure in our biblical lineage, was told to sacrifice his son. Throughout Scripture, men and women are provided with opportunities to choose obedience or disobedience. Consequences followed disobedience. But from the beginning of the scenario, God gave us the ability to choose.

Men of our day have been given the same choice. Some are blind to their self-destructive ways. Others are fully aware but choose not to be obedient. Their self-destructive tendencies destroy more than just themselves. It spills over into their businesses, their family, their ministries, and their lives.

Their blindness is like being trapped inside a burning house unaware. You see the commotion outside, but you cannot perceive the smoke and heat inside the building. You have a sense that something is wrong, but you cannot pinpoint exactly what it is.

I was once blind, but I am thankful that now I see. For example, my eating habits were terrible. They were absolutely terrible. Growing up in the South unearthed an endless possibility of eating unhealthy foods. I ate fried foods, desserts, overly salted food, and so much more daily. If what I saw seemed appetizing to my eyes, I ate it. I did not care. I became overweight quickly. I was totally ignorant of my self-destructive ways. It took constant rejection, an inability to perform simple exercises and an introduction to a healthier lifestyle for me to open my eyes to my unhealthy ways.

The blessed thing about having your eyes opened to the truth is your responsibility to believe and live out the truth you have heard. Yes, it is your responsibility to handle the truth wisely. Many believe it is what they know that makes the difference. Others believe it is who they know. Wise men believe it is what they choose to do with what they know and how they choose to interact with those they know that makes all the difference. There are other men who are too prideful to admit they are lost.

I was in a real internal struggle with admitting to my wife that we were lost. Sadly, I was willing to drive into a new state and lose precious time just so I could appear to know where I was going. That is pride, a lot of pride. Just think what happens when men do that throughout their lives. They go year after year moving in the wrong direction. They refuse to pull over and ask for help.

It sounds foolish, doesn't it? Yet men are living like this daily. Are you? Are you living a life that is clearly going in the wrong direction but you refuse to open your mouth and ask for help? If so, that is foolish and prideful.

I have encountered men who felt like asking for help made them appear weak. Men like to appear self-sufficient. They want others to think they know the right directions even if it is leading them right off a cliff. Being vulnerable is not something easy for many men to accept. Many of us look at life like it is an adventure. We do not want to be perceived as those who do not know how to win the battle, fight for the girl, score the winning point or defeat the evil boss. Some men have control issues, and they do not want to relinquish the control of going in a direction they perceive is right. Then, there are some men who have been made to think their way is not right.

I sat down with a couple some years ago. They were newly married, as was I. The wife was verbally abusive. She constantly told her husband how he was less of a man. It was sickening to watch and listen to her. Her husband had been emasculated to the point that he no longer believed he knew where he was going. He lost confidence in his ability to properly navigate the road he was meant to walk. He would tell me about opportunities in his household where his wife would dismiss his leadership and do just what she wanted. It got to the point that she drove their care because she convinced him that he always got lost. He stopped fighting her belittlement. He just gave in to all of it.

I will admit that some men do not need to lead anyone because they are headed straight for disaster. However, that is not the case for all of us. There are many of us who have a firm grasp of the vision God has given. We are willing and able to walk it out as He has directed us. But some men have a difficult time trying to reach a destination when they are yoked to a donkey.

The Bible tells us not to yoke a donkey and an ox together. The ox is considered a clean beast; the donkey is unclean. The ox is submissive and orderly; the donkey is very stubborn. When the donkey does not want to move, it does not. I watched a friend of my grandfather try many times to get a donkey to move when it did not want to move. He would leave it standing in the middle of the field. Finally the donkey would move when it was ready to.

The ox is a submissive animal that chooses to follow every command it is given. Can you imagine an ox being yoked together with a donkey? The ox would have no problem tilling the land like it is instructed, but the donkey would stop as soon as he decided he does not want to go. Can you imagine a marriage like that? Is your marriage like that? This is how some men feel in their marriages. They are trying to plow the field and go in the direction God is telling them to go, but their wives are not willing to budge. Some men feel like they are carrying dead weight. Get a visual of that. Visualize what it would look like to walk a mile with someone on your back. That is the situation many men find themselves in today.

Others are struggling with the expectation that they should know exactly where they are going, how they are going to get there, what they are going to use to get there, and what they are going to do when they get there.

If you are lost, seek help! Do not reject help when it is offered to you. And continue to trust in the help Jesus has provided for us through the Holy Spirit. He will guide you. Trust Him.

Chapter 13

Searching for Identity

"Cornelius, I do not know who I am." That is a common confession I hear men share. They do not know who they are, and that causes them to be silent. Many of these males are in search of purpose and identity. Anyone who is unclear about his purpose will often use what God gave him illegitimately.

We have a culture of males who were raised in single-parent households, mostly single mothers. A strong example of masculinity was missing in these households. They learned about masculinity from music, social media, books, and other males in their neighborhood. They were given a pattern for success, which was grade school, college, internships, and eventually a career. Many of them see the holes in that pattern and deviate from it. They want independence and they are willing to sacrifice everything to go in search of it. They desire something more than the status quo. They want to find who they are and what they have been called to do.

This process oftentimes leads them to be silent.

I met a man in his 50's who was finally tired of living the life others expected of him. He was successful in his own right. He had a great job with a generous benefits package. In fact, many of his investments made him a very wealthy man. After some soul-searching he resigned from his job.

He got the idea to plow his entire backyard. He enjoyed gardening but he never had time for it because he was constantly working. He and his wife had two children who were now living on their own. He lived with guilt and regret that he was not around to enjoy his children while they were young and at home. Now in mid-life, he wanted to find himself and discover his real purpose and to enjoy the things in life that brought him pleasure.

There are many men searching for answers. Their success is hampered because they are broken. They are fractured or damaged, and many have given up all hope. When you are broken, you will search for someone or something to put you back together. The righteous option, which is the only option for believers, is to run to God. We know that is not always the reality for most. Many run towards the world to indulge in worldly comfort and anything that satisfies their flesh. Because they saturate themselves in sin, they begin to identify with it. Those who begin to seek the world for healing will begin to live a life valuing attraction over principle; fantasy over faith; happiness over holiness.

In the search for answers and healing—because they are sick and diseased—many seek to numb the pain of the past with worldly narcotics instead of dealing with the issues of their heart and seeking comfort from the Holy Spirit. Many of these men have a form of godliness, but they deny the true power of it. And a form of godliness does not change the way we live. It allows us to set our own standards, claim they are acceptable to God, and live as if He is pleased with us. I have heard many men excuse their sin by saying, "I prayed about it, and God said it was okay." They twist scripture to condone their sin, and they find preachers that teach sermons that approve of their lifestyle. When confronted with the truth, they become angry because they love their sin more than they love God and His truth.

In their search for identity, many men have discarded the truth of the Word of God. Their hearts are numb to the truth. They are drugged up on worldly narcotics—that dulls their ability to recognize their sin. They have become addicted to temporary delight that ultimately leads to long-term, deadly consequences. Their rational thinking is dulled by alcohol, pills, heroin, morphine, pornography, strip clubs, morally degrading music, and overeating. They have a sweet tooth for sin, and they only indulge in sugary sermons.

Many have become apathetic—showing or feeling no interest, enthusiasm, or concern for their wellbeing or others. Some are numb to conviction and correction. They do not want to hear the truth anymore. They do not want to be held accountable. They want to eat, drink, and be merry. The motto for their lives is "you only live once" and therein lies their excuse for engaging in all kinds of sin. They saturate themselves in whatever they want to do. They live without standards or discipline. They are desensitized to the truth. In fact, they can hear the Word of God being preached but make no changes.

"Cornelius, I have heard this before!" "Cornelius, I know this already!" "I have been in church since I was a boy. I know the Bible!" These are just some of the excuses I receive from men. Could it possibly be that they know the Bible but have absolutely no connection with the Author—our holy God? Others have become irreverent about the things of God. They can sing the songs, play in the band, preach in the pulpit, but experience no power. They have a form of godliness, but they deny its power.

I know men who were once on fire for God. They gave the appearance that they were searching for identity in Him, but that changed suddenly. Instead, they are chasing their lustful passions. They are allowing pleasure-seeking to dictate their lifestyle. They use the excuse: "I was born this way." That is not something I can completely dispute. In fact, we were all "born this way"—into sin. This is why it is vital for all of us to be born again. God calls us to abstain, be disciplined, and pure, but the world encourages carnality, debauchery, and sensuality. This constant saturation in worldly lusts creates hardened hearts. People become blinded to the truth, cold-hearted, uncaring, and completely heartless towards others. Their blindness and intoxication with worldly things causes their family and community to fall apart. Their selfish indulgence is breaking down very foundational beliefs in society.

I have been in the company of pastors who admitted that preaching is no longer a passion for them; it is just a job. It is just another thing they do. They admit that they do not seek God in prayer on what should be taught. Instead, they search the internet for sermons taught by other preachers. They are not preachers; they are parrots. I am concerned for them, but I am more gravely concerned for those who sit under their teaching. My heart really goes out to them. Those who are under their care have not felt conviction in years. Some preach only what tickles the ear. They pervert the love of God and treat grace as if He is worthless and will accept sinful behavior.

In Romans 1:18-32, you will see how God gave men and women over to their lustful passions. They were allowed to indulge in their sin, and they had to suffer the consequences of their sin. Their destructive course brought great judgment. We see the judgment it brought in the days of Noah and in Sodom and Gomorrah. What is really heartbreaking is that we have the Bible to warn us of the dangers of sin. However, the people of Sodom and Gomorrah had no bibles. Because we have truth literally at our fingertips, one could only imagine the judgment reserved for those who do not repent. And I am very aware of the sacrifice of our Savior; however, His sacrifice was to draw us away from sin, not push us to indulge in it.

Sin strips man of his righteous identity. It destroys all peace of mind. It ruins marriages, families, and friendships. It has taken down many churches, destroyed legacies, and toppled great nations. I truly believe that very few people would indulge in their lustful behavior if the consequences of their actions were immediate.

There is one last concept of discovering identity I want to mention. I will explain it by examining the king of the jungle—the lion. He is ferocious and a formidable opponent. Every animal in the jungle is aware that it must be on its best behavior when the lion is around. His roar is mighty; claws are long and sharp, bite is deadly, and fight is until death. He is the king of his habitat. However, a lion is not so tough when he is placed in an unfamiliar environment. If placed in the Artic, he would have to either conform to his new environment or risk death. He would face new threats that would challenge his supremacy, and there stands a chance that he could be toppled as the ruler of his new territory.

Lions are king because they have learned to adapt to their surroundings. However, they are challenged when placed in a location that is not unfamiliar. I have encountered many men who are in search of identity who have wandered into new places and lost their confidence because they were unable to adapt to their new surroundings. They were strong and confident when they were living in the neighborhood where they grew up, working the same job from the time they were of age to start working, or engaged to a childhood sweetheart. But something changed in them when their environment changed. They were not able to make the adjustment properly; thus, they were lost in the shift.

Frank owned a trucking company for thirteen years. He found great success with it, but he started to lose clients after a competitor came in and offered rates he could not match. Frank had no other choice but to close his business. Needing to make money, he found a job working at a nearby lumber company. He had no other choice but to step outside of his comfort zone. His wife could feel his frustration. He was becoming much more testy and argumentative. The joy he once had was slowly dying away. She was trying everything she possibly could to figure out what was wrong with him, but he would not open up to her. All he continued to talk about was the business he lost. He was crushed by it.

His wife was so busy trying to get him to open up and talk that she was failing to listen to what he was saying. And there are many times that men talk about what is going on in their heart when they are fussing, nagging, or arguing. She felt like he would not quit fussing about the business he lost and the debt he was in. In her attempt to help him, she became frustrated. She began to notice how he would become more and more distant and quiet. She did not realize that he was dying inside and he refused to talk about it with her. He found himself in a different environment that required him to grow and develop. He was unwilling to make the adjustment in the role reversal of being the employee after so many years as an employer. What he had worked so hard to build and now lost cost him self-respect and confidence.

He and his wife divorced seventeen months after he lost his business. Frank never recovered. He soon found himself drinking every night to numb his emotional pain. Things really became dark for him.

You must know that God has not turned a blind eye to poor choices. Identity cannot be found in sin or a focus that eliminates God. Identity must be found in Him. Man. Husband. Father. Son. If you are a daughter, wife, or mother, I encourage you to pray for the men in your life. Pray that God will break and rebuild them as they surrender to Him.

Chapter 14

Just Trust Me

Britain was an ambitious man. He was a visionary full of fresh ideas that could generate multiple streams of income. Whenever I spent time with him, he would tell me he was trying to introduce a new product, invest in another property, or convince others to purchase a product he was promoting at the time. Unfortunately, he was never truly focused on one thing, and his wife grew tired of his random and multiple career tracks. He went from job to job looking for something to finally help him bring in the big dollars.

I spoke with him over lunch one afternoon and asked him about his marriage. He said his wife was threatening to leave him, and her reason was his instability. She thought highly of him in every other area except job stability. There were months when the lights and water in their home were cut off because of nonpayment. He was supposed to pay the bills; but instead he invested the money in another new product. She was working long hours to try to pay the bills. Her grace and patience were wearing thin. She could not help but feel that she was suffering as he chased his illusive dreams. She wanted her husband to finally wake up, face reality, and protect his home. I asked him what he said to her, and his words were: "Cornelius, I told her to just trust me."

This is a common theme I have found with many men who dare to dream and excel outside society's "norms." These men are leaders in their own way. They know their potential, and they refuse to settle for anything that is considered normal. They are the men who will do anything but live a life that is fixed on working solely to pay the bills. I know these men because I am one of them.

There are some men who live a life of fantasy, not faith. They put their families in financial situations that ultimately destroy their morale and confidence in his leadership. His spouse questions whether he can lead them out of their financial difficulties. He finds himself at a difficult crossroad. He will not settle for just any job or take up a trade to supplement his income. He realizes he has a family to feed.

I have seen men at this fork in the road. Some decide to conform to tradition by taking any job they can find. Others make the honorable decision to put their dreams on the back burner so their family can thrive. Some neglect their family's needs by continuing to chase their dreams. Some move on and abandon their families. Others convince their families to relocate to a different city where more opportunity is available. Still some invest all of their family's money and lose all of it. The family suffers greatly and the marriages suffer as well. Many of these couples divorce and the children are found in the difficult predicament of having to choose between their mother and their father.

I know what it is like to be a leader, and it is not easy. I believe it is righteous to give everyone in the home a voice. Yes, that means my children have a voice. They are people, and I want them to know their voice is powerful and worth honoring. Does that mean I will fulfill their unrighteous requests? Absolutely not, but I will listen to their thoughts and respond accordingly. This means I could have several opinions at one time, but I am tasked to make the right decision at the right time. Ultimately, the Spirit of God must lead me, and He must be reason for the decision I make.

Two months after my wife and I were married I told her that God had been dealing with me about resigning from my job. She understood, and she agreed. She saw how stressed I was. I was not myself. It was killing me. I had something else to tell her, but I was not sure how she was going to take it. I finally asked her what she thought about us moving to a different state. She was open to hearing what I had to say, but she was cautious. I finally came out and told her that I felt compelled to move to Mississippi. She looked at me and said, “Baby, I trust you.” Those words meant more to me than anything I could have imagined.

Those were the words Britain wanted to hear from his wife, and those are the words many husbands want to hear from their wives. I must admit that my wife’s trust was something I earned, and trusting me was something she was willing to do. There must be a healthy balance of both.

I did not realize it at the time, but a decision I made at the beginning of our courtship cemented a type of respect in my marriage that I yearned for and greatly desired. On our first outing, I told my wife that I would not kiss her until our wedding day. Initially, I felt the most important thing was not kissing her, but it truly was not. It was about honoring her as God's daughter and showing her that she could trust my words and follow my leadership. She would constantly remind me after we were married that it would have been difficult to follow me if I chose to go back on my word.

In fact, she once dated a guy who told her he would wait to kiss her on their wedding day. He broke that promise early on in the relationship. She said her respect for him and trust in his leadership took a nosedive. It ultimately led to the end of their relationship because she could not see herself being married to a man she did not respect.

Respect is important for men. And I believe that men should earn the respect they desire in their home by keeping their word, staying in communication, and taking care of their responsibilities.

If you are woman reading this book, I ask that you willingly trust instead of constantly nag about your man's ability to lead. I have seen situations where the men have abused their leadership and torn down more than they have built, which breaks the ability to trust. It can be hard to constantly give something to someone after they have continued to abuse it. However, I have seen men truly blossom because of the trust they received from their wives.

I believe the strength of a man can be found in his foundation, which must be Christ, and the support of his family. That makes Clark Kent, Superman. That makes Bruce Wayne, Batman. That transforms the most timid man into a strong and powerful being. There is nothing greater than a man and woman who come together on one accord. This strong bond is held together with constant communication that includes direction, encouragement, and purpose. Direction explains where the couple is headed, encouragement propels both of you to continue the journey, and purpose details the reason why the two of you must go in that particular direction. Communication that includes these three components strengthens the bond shared between the man and woman and promises a greater future for their family. Because the two agree in communication, it is easier for them to walk together.

Chapter 15

Renewing Your Mind

I want you to consider what it truly means to give your life to Christ. Imagine you are standing before Him having a game-changing conversation. It might would go something like this:

'Son, give me your life.'

'Okay Jesus, you can have it! But how much of it do you want? Do you also want even some of my very expensive belongings?"

'Yes, I want those things, too. I want all of them. What else do you have?'

'I have a few dollars in my pocket right now.'

'I want that, too. Is that all you have?'

'No, I have a house.'

'Okay, I want the house.'

'But Jesus, if I give you the house I will be forced to live in my RV!'

'You have a RV? Great; I want that too.'

'But if you take my RV and home I will be forced to live in my car! Where will my wife and children sleep? You took my money! How will we

eat? I will have hardly anything after I give you those things.'

'Oh, so you have a car too? Give me that as well. And you mentioned you had a wife and children. I want them too. What else do you have?'

'That is it! I have nothing left. You took everything from me.'

'No, you have not given Me everything. There is one more thing I want—YOU! I will allow you to use all the things you have now, but you must always remember that they are Mine just as you are Mine. When I call for them, you must freely give them up for they belong to Me, as you belong to Me.'

You probably realize by now that the decision to follow Jesus is costly. It requires everything that you have, everything you are and everything you will become. Many men look at what it truly means to give their lives to Christ and become intimidated. They think the process is more than they can handle. They see themselves as unworthy and unable to fully give themselves away to Christ, and they are absolutely right.

Jesus did not die for perfect men. He did not come to make bad men good; He came so dead, imperfect men might live through Him. He fully expects for you to bring all of your worries, cares, past, and baggage to the cross and leave it there. He expects for you to be reborn through Him. And this process of rebirth requires a process of renewing your mind.

I tried to play several sports when I was growing up. Unfortunately, I was not good at anything. In fact, I was terrible at everything. I did learn a few things though. One of the most important things I learned was that I could not expect to play a different game using another game's rules. For example, I could not expect to be good at basketball if I chose to play by the rules for football. I had to choose which set of rules I would use and play the game I was involved in at that moment. This principle also applies to our life as Christian men.

We cannot expect to be a follower of Christ while living by the same expectations and rules we learned from the streets, the club, the field, the court, the alley, or the backyard or what we learned from the adoptive parent, the group home parent, or that one crazy uncle. The process of renewing your mind is not a difficult one, but it does take a great deal of patience, humility, and a desire to change.

Jesus did not leave us helpless when He ascended to sit at the right hand of the Father. He provided the Holy Spirit to dwell with us. He does not speak anything outside of what Jesus has already said. He convicts us to holiness and constantly pleads the case for righteousness. He guides, teaches, convicts, and comforts us.

I want you to consider what your life would be like if Jesus was with you daily. Would you still do the same things you do now? Would you have more of an urgency to share the Gospel with the lost? Would you desire to give more to the local church and care for the widows and orphans? Would you sleep as much as you do; eat as much as you do; entertain yourself with television as much as you do? I am sure there are many things about your life you would change. Just the reality of having Jesus with us in the flesh would be a little overwhelming for some.

I am convinced that many Jesus-followers would not follow Him today. They would assume His message of purity is too harsh. I am sure He would be shunned in the media for not being politically correct. He would create such a firestorm of emotions that would quickly bring unprecedented conviction to all who follow Him. His presence would truly separate the sheep from the goats; the tares from the wheat.

Most fail to realize that the Holy Spirit being with us is just like Jesus being with us. Jesus appeared in flesh; the Holy Spirit is not of flesh. He is a Spirit. His being cannot be perceived with the human eye. However, His presence is powerful and His influence can be seen in our new actions. The fruit of the Spirit—written about in Galatians 5—is evidence of His presence. I know I have been changed in my heart because of my new actions. My desires have changed. I no longer desire to do the things I once loved. I desire something different; something special; something with an eye on eternity. I desire to live a life that is pleasing to God. I did not have that mindset before. He gave me a desire to change and renew my mind.

I believe you have that desire simply because you are reading this book. Men who seek out information do it so they can change and grow. I always recommend that men ask the Holy Spirit for a desire to change.

I knew men who were once on fire for God. They were so joyful and excited about the things of the Lord. They went downtown in Atlanta to share the Gospel in the parks and near some of the tourist attractions. Their excitement was so contagious that it encouraged me to do more. However, I have seen a change in them over the years. They have grown cold about the things of God. They are not as joyful as they once were. Talking to them is very difficult because they question God's ability, though they once proclaimed His glory and ability to do all things. These men had a strong desire to change, but like a flickering flame, the light begins to burn out quickly. I would assume that their desire began to fade because they were excited about doing the works of the Lord, but they lost focus on truly spending time with the Lord of the works. They became busy about activity instead of focusing on intimacy with Him. They were doing so much for Him, but without spending quality time with Him. And I believe many believers today have grown tired from all the works they do for God that they forget to actually take time to sit in His presence and experience Him in prayer, Bible reading, fasting, and meditating on Scripture.

As a friend of those guys, I felt it was my responsibility to confront them about their coldness towards God. I encouraged them to cry out to Him and ask Him to return the joy they lost. The guys took a sabbatical for two weeks. They went off in the woods to just fast and pray. They wanted to encounter God again. The men came back from their trip truly renewed.

Did I believe their salvation was sure the first time? Absolutely. Although this time it was like they were born again, again. Their salvation was sure; however, God restored and renewed that passionate flame that had slowly dimmed because of worldly influences. They were new men with the right focus. They had a renewed mind to seek God, not do a lot of things for Him. They had to learn that their activity is birthed out of their identity. Who they are will reveal what they do. And they are God's men, so they seek Him first for the assignments. Then they perform them as He directs.

Those men needed their minds and hearts to be renewed. You need the same thing. I need the same thing. We all need it. Renewal of the mind is an ongoing process. It does not end. There is always more for us to learn. The important thing is to focus in on the Teacher, not the lesson. The Teacher, who is the Holy Spirit, will guide you through the lesson.

I know the concept of having the Holy Spirit lead and teach you can seem a little farfetched to some. I do not want you to think of it as a difficult thing to conceive. Consider His presence like that of Jesus being with you. Also consider spending time with Him just like you would spend time with Jesus if He were standing before you. You would not try to hide. You would be direct and willing to listen to what He says.

Take that same approach when you sit with the Holy Spirit. Ask Him questions. Ask Him to give you a desire to change and open you up your family's sake. Ask Him to burn everything inside of you that is not like Him. I spent years of my life going to God for answers. I asked Him a lot of questions, but I was not doing one very important thing—sitting down to listen. I needed to hear what He had to say, but I did not make time to listen. Do not make that same mistake. Go to God with the intention to talk, listen, and obey.

Chapter 16

The Lust Hook

I have written about lust in all of my books. It is a subject that must be discussed, and we must know that we have been set free from its bondage through Jesus.

Many men are silent because they are currently engaged in a very real battle with sexual lust. The most common activities associated with sexual lust for many men are watching pornography or being involved in sexual promiscuity. It is the hook that captures a man before it takes him so low that he drowns. It starts off as a desire to fulfill his curiosity. He fails to recognize that one-minute of watching that perversion will place him in real bondage. It will play in his head like a movie. It will haunt him wherever he goes, bother him when he tries to do something, throw off his concentration when he is trying to sit still and make him think that he is not capable of overcoming his bondage.

It is a hook that takes a man so deep that he slowly removes his boundaries one by one. For example, he will start doing things he said he would never do like drive an hour to an adult novelty shop to purchase certain DVDs, visit pornographic websites on his lunch break, reach out to men and women through dating sites, and start emotional relationships with people other than his wife. He will begin to indulge in all the things that once disgusted him. I have encountered men who found themselves in destructive situations because they were hooked on the lust they craved from watching pornography. Some of them were caught having sex with animals. Some were caught having sex with other men. Some were caught having sex with multiple women. They were indulging in things they said they would never do.

The hook of lust lured them from the shore of safety into a deep, dark world of impossibility, danger, and death. Many men have flirted with this hook only to drown. Some have been able to escape the hook, but the damage was done. They came back to the shore with sexually transmitted diseases that ultimately cost them their lives. Some men have taken others down into the depths of the sea of lust with them.

There is a concept about lust I want you to understand. It is not something you fall into; it is something that grows within you. Perversions grow within you. If you continue to feed them, they will grow. You will find yourself doing things and indulging in things you said you would never entertain. It is the same concept as starting a fire. If you constantly add fuel to the fire, it will continue to grow until it burns everything in its path. And it will burn everything.

I have seen homes torn apart because of a pornography addiction. For many spouses, it is an issue of trust. When she catches her husband watching pornography she sees it as him hiding something from her, which it is. She does not care that he has a serious addiction. She is concerned that her husband is engaging in something privately that he could not let her know about publically. His inability to talk to her about it crushes her. It makes her question what else he might be hiding from her. It makes her question her ability to fulfill her husband's desires. The weight of mistrust can reach a point where the marriage ends.

I have spoken with many couples who have experienced this issue in their marriage. A wife suspected her husband of engaging in pornography. He was always up late at night, locking the bathroom door, desiring to travel to certain places alone, and always keeping his phone close. Her suspicions were correct. She caught him one night after following him to the bathroom. He did not lock the door because he thought she was asleep. After discovering him in the act of masturbation and watching pornography, she was crushed. She wept and grew angry. He tried to make excuses for his actions. She scolded him.

I have never believed that harsh and demeaning words are effective in this or any type of situation. It is best to recognize the problem, which is lust and perversion, and deal with it. It is best to go to God in prayer, find Spirit-filled counselors, find brothers to hold you accountable, and set up proper boundaries so this does not happen again. Discouraging someone does not change his heart; it pushes him away because he knows he cannot live up to someone else's expectations.

I encountered one couple where the wife found out about the husband watching pornography and masturbating. She was crushed because she could not understand why she was not enough to satisfy him. She continued to question why he felt like he needed something or someone other than her. It got to the point that she felt unworthy and her self-esteem suffered greatly because of it. They are married today, but their marriage is not the same. God is still working on her heart and identity within their marriage.

Another wife found her husband watching pornography. He told her that he was just trying to learn how to satisfy her. He also manipulated her into watching it with him to improve their sex life. He twisted Hebrews 13:4, which reads "Marriage is to be held in honor among all, and the marriage bed is to be undefiled; for fornicators and adulterers God will judge." He encouraged her to believe that the bed being undefiled meant they could do whatever they wanted to do because they were married. He did not care about her comforts or needs.

His desire was to fulfill his lusts he developed from years of watching pornography. She found herself supporting his lustful habits and desires because he made her believe that she was not a true submissive wife unless she did exactly what he wanted her to do. That, my friend, is not submission; that is slavery. Submission is willful and righteous; slavery is forced and unrighteous. The husband soon grew tired of her and he started seeking sex from women on dating sites. After his third encounter with a woman he met on a dating site, he discovered he contracted a sexually transmitted disease. He made his wife think she was infected some other way and was the one who infected him. Lust controlled him, he controlled his marriage, and all of it destroyed the purity of their union. Their marriage bed was no longer pure and undefiled. It was filled with hurt, deceit, disease, and manipulation.

Men who are engaged in a battle with pornography become cowards, because sin makes men cowards. I have met men, especially preachers, who will not speak on the topic with passion because they are being defeated by it daily. And I have met men, especially preachers, who choose to dismiss it like it is not important and dangerous. They become dangerous men who are willing to drink poison and sell it to others. They indulge in sexual promiscuity, put on a show of integrity, and then preach to others as if they have it together. I have never wanted that to be my reality because I know I am still a work in progress. However, I refuse to give in or give up. I know the satisfaction from lust is not worth the consequences.

Lust destroys a man's confidence in himself and the truth he claims to believe. He begins to think he is a bad, unworthy person because of his addiction. Although he believes in true freedom he cannot escape the strong grip lust has on him. He begins to think no one loves him or that no one would truly love him if they really knew him privately. He battles a real question in his head: Would anyone follow me if my private life was put on public display? Many men are privately miserable today because they cannot escape the fact that they are living a life as a public success, but they know they are private failures. Their private actions will one day show in their public performance.

Because they think no one will love them because of their private actions, they will do one of two things—hide their sin or hide themselves. They will anticipate rejection and continue a destructive and self-perpetuating cycle of addictive behavior. This cycle reinforces their belief that no one loves them. This keeps them insecure and gives them reason to remain hidden from the world. They put on masks and do things like hide themselves in work, professional titles, academic degrees, financial earnings, sexual partners, and even their spiritual gifts. Many develop reprobate hearts and quench the truth to continue living in their sin. Titus 1:16 reads "They profess to know God, but by their deeds they deny Him, being detestable and disobedient, and worthless for any good deed." These men's minds harden to the truth, and their faith becomes corrupted. They claim to know God, but their works do not prove their faith. They claim to serve our holy God, but their actions are far from holy. They gather with preachers who will tell them what they want to hear. They run from any discipline and correction. They are led by their own desires and wishes. They do not have a desire to please God. They suppress the truth with their wickedness.

Some begin to think that no one can really meet their needs. They begin to idolize the idea of self-satisfaction. They fall into the habit of masturbation. Many soon grow bored with the images and videos. They desire the real touch of another person.

The craving becomes so strong that they run to get whatever will satisfy their perverse desires. They get to a point of seeking whatever their eyes desire. They begin to think their addiction is their greatest need, so they think they cannot quit. They are hooked on lust and drowning in perversion.

Their private lustful actions begin to affect their public performance. There are many preachers, singers, doctors, lawyers, CEO's, and other men with fancy titles who foster a strong sense of hypocrisy because they know their private actions are wrong. Luke 8:17 reads "*For nothing is hidden that will not become evident, nor anything secret that will not be known and come to light.*" Those are convicting words of truth that cannot be ignored or pushed away. Men around the world know of their hypocrisy, but they continue to act as if nothing is wrong. Is that you? Are you doing the same thing? If so, you must know that the truth will be revealed. The blanket you are using to cover your actions will be lifted, and your private actions will be revealed.

I encourage you to confess those things going on in your life right now. Uncover those perverse actions. Let the light of Christ shine on them by confessing Him as Savior and Lord. Ask the Holy Spirit to fill your heart and give you reverence for God that restrains you from the sin He hates. Ask Him to grow the fruit of self-control in your life. Ask Him to do whatever is necessary to remove the hook of lust in your life. He will do it. I know He will do it. He did it for me.

If you are living in lust or know a man who is currently trapped in a hook of lust, I encourage you to pray for him. Pray that God will expose his actions. Encourage him to come out of his perversion, and refuse to make him comfortable when he is around you. Do not allow him to think his actions are acceptable. This does not mean you condemn him. Honestly, his actions are enough condemnation. Not making him comfortable means you continue to have certain standards even though he has lost all of his.

I want you to imagine a forest filled with trees as far as your eyes can see. There is a little boy in the forest towards the edge of it. He has a match in his hand. Curiosity and youthful enthusiasm leads him to light the match. The small flame begins to quickly run down the short wick of the match until it reaches his fingertips. In a moment's notice, he drops the lit match. The small flame begins to spread by feeding on the leaves and debris that is on the ground of the forest floor. The small flame is now growing larger and larger as it begins to devour everything in its path. The boy looks on as what was once a small flame has transformed into a raging fire that he cannot control. He is helpless to stop the fire from destroying the entire forest and everything else in its path. Although he recognizes the destruction, he continues to light other matches. With each match, he says it will be the last one he lights, but he continues to go back over and over again.

Feeling hopeless, now on his knees, he calls out for help. His heart is pure. In the distance a man appears and quenches the flames. The fire is put out, but the destruction has been done. Acres and acres of trees have been burned to the ground. Homes were destroyed. Lives were lost and ruined. And no one would have ever thought all of that could come from a small flame.

I was that little boy. Many men today can relate. Our curiosity, youthful enthusiasm, natural inclination towards sin, and a strong surge of testosterone flowing through our masculine body led us to test the boundaries of sex. It became a small exploration to discover all the things we think we wanted and needed. We did not think we would be held captive by the sex we chose to explore, but it soon became our master. It began to rule us. And like the small flame quickly traveling down the wick of the match, lust began to fill our heart. It became too hot to hold on to and handle. We had no other choice, but to let it go. We had to watch it fall. Then we watched as it began to grow as we fed it.

Each time we watched pornography we were burning down another tree of innocence and feeding the flame of lust. Another tree was destroyed each time we actively unzipped our pants to satisfy ourselves with masturbation; a house was ruined. We were slowly losing a grip on our sexuality and purity. We were hooked on something that was destroying us. It was destroying everything in its path without any regard for who would suffer. Each sexual experience was another forest burned down; another soul tied to ours; another lost opportunity to deny temptation and do the right thing.

Each tree represents a part of our lives and innocence that was burned away because we watched and engaged the flame of lust as it slowly overcame the community around us.

Once the small flame feeds on enough leaves and debris it

transforms into something we never thought we would encounter—a raging fire. The fire becomes so overwhelming that we cannot see a way of escape. We see the destruction before us. We see the damaged homes, ruined self-esteem, disobedience to God's Word and desire for purity, and so much more, but we continue to indulge in it. We continue to light more matches!

Finally we give in and realize we cannot stop this raging fire of lust burning within us. When we ask for help, Jesus appears and stops the flames from destroying anything else in its path. When He tells it to stop, it stops—IMMEDIATELY!

We have a sense of relief, but we notice the destruction it has caused. It has ravaged our lives and taken the people we love captive. Many homes were destroyed because of it. Marriages were ruined. Children found the matches we were playing with and began to light them without us knowing. They found the magazines under the bed, clicked on the pornographic internet addresses in the history of the computer, and grew to indulge in the things we wished they would have stayed away from. They have lit their own matches, and we are unaware of the generational destruction we have caused. We are responsible for those who lit their matches from our flames of lust. Choosing not to go back to help those who are struggling and lost in how to quench the fire makes you an accomplice in their destruction. How many men will light their matches with our lustful flame? How many have you led astray?

But Jesus quenches the flames. He pulls us back on to the shore. He takes the hook from out of our mouths. He takes our repented sin and tosses it into the sea of forgetfulness and remembers it no more. He provides us with Help, which is the Holy Spirit, to refrain from indulging in that sin again. He restores all that was lost in the fire and gives new life to all that was destroyed in the flames.

Do not stay silent any longer. Your silence is causing mass destruction. You cannot keep it hidden. It must be revealed. Cry out to Jesus and confess Him as Savior and Lord. He has come to our rescue! He has come to save us from the fires we have lit and to deliver us from the hook that has taken us into the depths of the sea of perversion and lust. We must trust Him and lean on Him.

Chapter 17

The Emasculation of Men

Silence is the absence of sound. To be silent is to be completely quiet.

Some have said that the best response to criticism you could offer critics is your silence. While there is some truth in that statement, it is not something that is recommended. Communication can be inaudible, but those with the ability to speak should open their mouths to say what needs to be said. The problem with many of our men in our society today is they have perfected the art of silence. Many practice the "silent treatment" for many reasons.

Our society championed the cause of women's rights in significant ways. The Preamble of the Constitution of the United States is very eloquent. Its beginning reads "We the people..." When that document was signed on September 17, 1787, women were not granted many of the liberties they have today. Their abilities were limited; status was suppressive. In short, women were not included in that "We the people..." Although the United

States was founded upon freedom from oppression we quickly became a country that became synonymous with suffrage and oppression, especially for women and people of color. But through the process of amendment, public voting, court decision, and common sense, people of color and women were finally included in "We the people..."

The Constitution was ratified on August 18, 1920 to grant American women the right to vote. Many of their social liberties were granted many years afterwards. Now, women enjoy many of the same social, economic, and legal privileges as male citizens. Now, married women can own property and legally claim any money that is earned in the household. In fact it is not uncommon to see a woman making the bulk of the money in the household. Women were once relegated to being homemakers caring for the home and the children--two very distinct privileges that have caused a controversy today.

In our haste to upgrade the social status, roles, and responsibilities of women, we have almost forgotten about the social status, responsibilities, and roles of men. The fight to keep women and men equal has created a large gap in the relationship between men and women. I applaud how far we have come to properly define the roles and privileges of women; however, I do not condone the way we have belittled the God-given roles of the man and the woman.

God purposed for the man to lead, to guide, to cultivate, to be fruitful, to multiply, to subdue, and to rule. The woman was created to help. She is the weaker vessel. Her beauty is matchless.

She is graceful, nurturing, and gentle. In the rush to properly define women's roles, we have belittled the God-given responsibilities for both man and woman. Many compare the roles of men and women and call the disparity unfair; however, the process of comparing one with the other runs the risk of belittling one over the other.

Women are powerful in the way God ordained and created them. Men are powerful in our own way. Our leadership, as men, should be founded on love and grace. Because many ungodly men have stood to lead, women have been forced to bear the burden of hatred and self-described oppression. Some men use violence and fear to keep women suppressed.

The Bible is also filled with a great deal of women's suffrage; however, ungodly men enacted most of those actions. Our leadership became dominant and deadly. While I stand to applaud the steps we have made in the rights of men and women, I cannot help but look upon our society today and notice how our women and young girls are encouraged to take a role of leadership and authority God did not give them.

Women are called the keepers of the home. Nowadays, women are strongly encouraged to ignore the home and run the boardroom. Is this to say women cannot run a boardroom? Absolutely not. But it is wrong to suggest that women should seek the boardroom at the expense of their families. The thought of having children has almost been cast aside in the minds of many women. For many of them, their ambition to be better than a man has become very costly for men and little boys all around the world.

I am not trying to define roles with this book; the Bible has already done that. However, I want to paint a very distinct line between the differences in men and women. Men and women are equal in the way we were created; however, our roles are different. And being different is not a bad thing. Because of our differences, one is able to bring proper balance to the other. When we submit and fall in line with our different purposes, we are able to bring a balanced approach to the way we live and govern our household. An inability to do that brings chaos and disorder. It has also blurred the lines of responsibilities in our society today. Men do not know how to be men and women do not know how to be women. Many are chasing a two-headed system that is running straight to disaster. Anything with more than one head is a monster.

God is orderly. The Father is the head of Jesus, Jesus is the head of man, man is the head of woman and woman is the head, or keeper, of the household, which includes the children. Many progressives disagree with this God-ordained order, but our inability to follow it will bring more chaos, confusion, and disorder.

I have encountered men who have been so confused about their proper role in the home and in society that they have almost given up trying. They do not excel at anything because they have grown comfortable in believing that women can usurp their authority and take their place. While I do not agree that a woman's place is to be barefoot and pregnant, I believe the idea of that concept has created a firestorm of controversy.

We have allowed the intellect of some male chauvinists to become the thoughts of all men. Because of this, many men are fighting so hard to agree and champion the "supreme, independent woman" that they have lost all identity in who they were created to be. The woman works so hard to be independent until she figures out that she hates to be alone. Her independent mind leads her to choose singleness, and it is not good for the man or woman to be alone. Many women are so intent on being the head of the household that they want to make the bacon, bring it home, cook it, and devour it all by themselves.

At some point, a woman wakes up to find out that she is single and lonely. Others are climbing the social ladder of success but their husbands, children, and home have to suffer because of her absence. While I understand her ability to do everything and appear as a modern-day Wonder Woman, I cannot help but see the destruction of our families being rooted in women no longer wanting to keep their home, love their husbands, and care for their children. Instead, it has turned into a dangerous fight, and both women and men are losing.

The young man is conflicted about the idea of trying to lead an independent woman. That is like trying to lead a ravenous lion down the Sahara without any restraints or order. Sooner or later, the lion will run or eat the man. And many men have become lunch to women. Like the Black Widow, she gets what she wants from men then eats him for her nourishment.

I have sat down with many wives who say their husbands

act like he has nothing to say. Most times, it is because the man has been emasculated. He has been mentally, socially, and sometimes, physically stripped of his God-given masculinity. And while our society works hard to upgrade the social status of women, our men are still expected to be men. In any relationship, someone is going to have to bend the knee and submit. Unfortunately, it looks like men are taking that action so it does not ruffle women's feathers. It is a tactic that has been employed since the beginning of time when the serpent went to Eve in the Garden of Eden instead of going to Adam.

Many men have nothing to say.

In many situations, it is true that men feel as if they have nothing to say. It is also true that many men have something to say, but some have no confidence in what they want to say. They have been convinced that they should not believe in their own words. There are many organizations, conferences, seminars and programs aimed at uplifting and instilling confidence in women, but where are those same programs for men?

As a pastor I find it difficult to get men to talk about things other than sports, money, food, and women. Our men's ministry is a fraction of the size of the women's ministry. My wife has a yearly conference where women gather from all over the world. Her first year more than 800 women attended. The second year brought more than 1,400 women. The numbers continue to mushroom. On the other hand, I have held a men's conference that is on the same dynamic level as the women's conference. We have yet to break the 100-man mark. Trying to get men together is like trying to shepherd a herd of bulls.

When I finally gather men in one place I encourage them to speak. Unfortunately, many of them have absolutely nothing to say. They have grown silent. They are emasculated to the point of complete silence. They are either the product of a verbally abusive wife or mother. They have been told to be quiet so much that they took those words seriously. They were not given a place to freely express their masculinity and explore the world they have been given to cultivate and rule. They are like caged lions that have been locked away for many years. These men feel less than men, and many times, they are still basing the present reality on past mistakes.

Women must be careful about assuming a position as an ultimate authority. In an effort to be the man's equal in all things, she robs him of his masculinity and headship. Women have a very important role in the success of men. Because they were made to help, the enemy uses them to hurt. And nothing is worse than having the one who is created to help you, hurt you. A woman's influence can build the confidence of men. A woman's encouragement, especially the encouragement of a man's wife, can set the tone for his success. Encouraging him is like pouring courage in his heart and strengthening him to continue to fight for the wellbeing of his community and family.

When a woman undermines her husband, he cannot operate from a place of confidence and courage. Discouragement takes courage out of him. Her discouraging words drain him of his full strength. We must remember that we as men are yoked together with women. We are in this together. We have the ability to influence one another. And with great influence comes an even greater responsibility.

What are things that women do to emasculate men?

Belittle him publically.

I do not believe I have ever met a man who was not angered at the thought of being publically humiliated. It is one thing to be disrespected at home. It is totally different to be disrespected in front of others. It is the ultimate form of disrespect and humiliation.

I have encountered several men whose wives insist on destroying their character around other people. They are the couple who makes everyone else uncomfortable. She tears him down with her words. In an attempt to keep the peace, he bites his tongue. He is afraid to speak in front of her because he does not know what she is going to say about him. He is emotionally and mentally abused by the woman he has promised to spend the rest of his life with. He lives every day regretting their marriage and in fear of her wrath-filled words. And the nightmare only heightens when things turn violent. She is aware that if he puts his hands on her, he will go to jail. She uses that against him. She throws things at him, hits him, and threatens to call the police any moment he appears to move towards her in an aggressive manner. He feels helpless because he does not want anyone outside of his marriage to know his wife is abusing him. His ego keeps from speaking.

While at dinner with one couple the server came to get our meal orders. He had already brought our drinks to the table. My wife and I ordered our food. The server asked the other couple for their order, but the husband started to ask a question about the menu. Before he could finish, his wife blurted out, "Excuse me! I am the woman; therefore, I order first. Did your momma teach you anything? You are such an idiot. Stop doing stupid stuff." She then looked at the server and apologized for her husband's behavior and placed her order. I took a sip of my water, looked at my wife, and gave her the death stare. She looked at me and shook her head. The husband sat there silently with his head bowed.

It was apparent that this was not the first time he was humiliated publically. He was so used to it that he did not have a response. Having to witness that public castration was difficult for me. I wanted to respond for him, but I knew that speaking up for him could very well emasculate him even more. It would be disrespectful for me to correct his wife for her outlandish behavior. And the last thing I wanted to do was disrespect him more. Instead, I chose to wait until my wife and I were alone to discuss their marriage. I can understand if he was going ahead of her to order his food, but that was not the case. He was asking a question.

After the wife finished her tirade, she looked at my wife and began to tell her about how men do not know how to treat a woman. I could not do anything but laugh. Her hypocrisy was appalling. I wondered if she recognized what she was doing to her spouse by publically belittling him. I could only imagine what kind of verbal abuse he endured at home.

As the dinner continued, the husband contributed very little to our dinner conversation. He responded when I spoke to him, but not much beyond that. Before he spoke, he would glance over at his wife as if he needed her approval. Every word he said was being monitored. I did not envy him at all. I wondered if she knew what she was doing to him. The husband did not have many options. He could run from the situation, but some would say he is not being strong responding like a man. He could just be cool, calm, and lower his head. Or he could yell back at her and be seen as insensitive. He was placed in a difficult spot. If he does not find a solution and address the problem soon, he will grow completely silent to avoid upsetting his wife. That is no way for a man to live.

Belittle his occupation.

We live in a society where some women are the primary breadwinners. That means they make more money than their husbands. Many fail to understand that marriage is about unity. The man and woman cease being individuals; they come together as one. Their salaries are not as important as what they do with their collective resources as a couple.

I have encountered several marriages where the wife is critical of her husband's occupation and salary. One wife in particular said, "Cornelius, all he makes is $56,000 a year! I make

$70,000." I was not sure what she was trying to gain by sharing that information with me. In fact, $56,000 is a salary I know many men would love to have. I couldn't resist reminding her that people can lose their high-paying jobs as quickly as they gain them.

Early on in my marriage, I did not work a regular 9 to 5 job and my wife worked from home. During an argument, she started to belittle my inability to bring a certain amount of money into the household. I knew what God told me to do, and I was doing the very best I could to provide for my family while being obedient to him. Her words hurt me deeply. I know she made the remarks in a moment of anger. I said some really harsh things as well.

We stopped the arguing long enough for both of us to pray. While she was praying, the Holy Spirit began to really minister to her. He cautioned her about her attitude and reminded her that there is always the potential for losing a job. He told her to humble herself or risk being humbled. She quickly asked for my forgiveness and repented to God. Thankfully, we did not have to experience that again.

Often people think the more prestigious the job, the greater the man can claim to be. I have never heard a boy say he wanted to be a janitor or a garbage collector when we grew up. I am not saying there is anything wrong with those occupations. However, there are infinitely more little boys who want to be a doctor, an astronaut, or a dentist than those who want to flip burgers at the local burger joint. Most men aspire to do whatever will bring in the most prestige, money, and honor.

My aspiration was to become president of the United States. But today I am more content being a preacher. The president serves in the White House; a preacher is honored to serve in God's house. I will take the latter any day. I also wanted to have a corner office in a skyscraper. I wanted a large desk with my name on the door. I wanted a prominent title to boost my ego. I wanted all those things because I associated them with being important. When I finally landed those things, I realized they didn't bring me the satisfaction I was seeking after all.

I remember walking into my corner office in the bustling business district of downtown Atlanta. I felt like I made it. 'Look at me, everyone! I am important. My office, my business cards, my reserved parking space, my secretary at my beck and call. I had arrived, right? Wrong!

After a very short time in that position, I started to miss my newborn son. I wanted to live my life on my terms and that meant not being stuck in an office all day. I would look out the window and people watch. I saw families out strolling and enjoying the nice Atlanta breeze while I sat there in an office convincing myself that I was important. I could not do it any longer.

I packed up my belongings and left. I went home, picked up my son, and went to the park. I did not want life to continue passing me by while I chased something I did not really want or need. I was becoming an empty suit walking around with a nametag so others could identify me.

I was in a position to walk out of the office and make my

office at home in a less controlled environment. I am able to do it because I am the owner and operator of my businesses. Many men do not have that luxury. Some have to take whatever they can get to provide for their families.

Micromanage him.

One of the biggest problems with men being micromanaged is the way it chips away at their ego. I have seen so many men whose every move is criticized as if nothing they do is ever good enough. And many men base their worth on what they do. When what they do is not enough then they feel as if *they* are not enough. Micromanagement causes a man to grow silent. He loses his motivation to do anything. His initiative to try new things plummets. He becomes a dead man walking who is waiting for his time on earth to expire.

Ignore his advice after asking for it.

Before my wife and I were married, I was in a relationship where the woman loved to ask me for my advice. I would take the time to explain in detail what I thought was best. But did she hear me? Actually, she did the exact opposite of what I recommended. We were not bound by a covenant relationship of marriage so she wasn't obligated to listen to me or do what I suggested. But her complete disregard for what I shared really hurt me. I began to question if my words were important enough to listen to or take into consideration. I felt like what I was saying was worth hearing. Unfortunately, I felt like no one was listening.

What hurt the most was the fact that she came to me for advice. I didn't force it on her. Each time she dismissed my opinion, I felt less and less of a man. I felt like my words did not matter. Emasculation can truly deflate a man's ego.

What is probably worse than being ignored by woman when you offer advice is when she asks another man to do something or to give the advice on the same thing.

A husband approached me one evening and was clearly upset. After calming him down, he said, "Cornelius, I've told her to do the same thing over and over again, but she took her father's advice! The same advice that I gave her was meaningless until her daddy told her to do it." I believe he had every right to be upset. There are men who might demand that his way is the only way, but most men just want their opinions to at least be considered. In this husband's eyes, his wife chose her father's opinion over his. Doing this made the husband feel like his wife chose her father over him. It cut him deeply.

Another husband I was developing a relationship with appeared to suddenly become more and more distant. I could not understand what was going on. I finally had an opportunity to approach him. When I confronted him about the change in his behavior, he said he was upset with me. I was shocked because I couldn't recall what I could have done to make him so angry.

He explained that he and his wife were arguing one day when she blurted out, "That is not what pastor said!" He said the argument got heated, and his wife continued to try to correct him by telling him what I said in my sermon. After allowing him to finish explaining himself, I had to point out a very fundamental fact. Not only was I not in his home or involved in their argument, but I did not know what was going on between them. He apologized to me, and our relationship has been better ever since. However, what his wife did is what I believe has caused many men to dislike the man in the pulpit. His wife discredited his words by valuing the preacher's words more. This is the height of emasculation.

I encouraged that couple and other couples to make sure they did not use the pastor's words in an argument. My role is to preach the Word of God. My words must mirror His words. Therefore, it is best for the couple to use the same Word of God that is my source to resolve their problems. I could only imagine the hurt the man felt when his wife chose to bring another man into their discussion. I did not know I was being brought into the picture to help her try to "win" an argument.

Men can be very territorial. Like the lion that guards his kingdom, men protect whatever has been placed in their care and whatever they believe is valuable. This is why it is normal for a man to be seen as a protector. One key thing to remember about men is that we guard what we value. Women who want to know what a man values should pay close attention to what he guards or protects.

If he is hiding something, it is a strong indication that he fears what he values will be taken if it is exposed. The risk of exposure is too heavy a price to pay. Hiding becomes his solution, and it becomes his method of protecting what he values. If a man notices that someone continues to rob him of what he values then he will either try to hide it or destroy whatever is trying to come against him and whatever he values.

Men who are discredited and criticized constantly tend to withdraw into silence. They guard their words as a defensive mechanism to avoid hurt. Some men use sarcasm or negative words to deflect the hurt on others. Their goal is to protect their territory.

When a husband does not honor his marriage, he will not make an effort to salvage it. If he feels that he or his words are being dismissed by his wife, he will begin to assume that he has nothing valuable to bring to the relationship. He may resort to using sarcasm and other unrighteous speech instead of thinking before he responds. When a man succumbs to defeat by feeling he is not valued, the only cure for this man is a regular dose of encouragement. It adds value to him and to his relationships.

Chapter 18

Intimidated

I was approached by a teenager at church who inquired about assistance for the homeless. After a brief discussion, I found out that he was homeless. I could sense the hurt and pain in his heart. As I began to comfort and encourage him, he began to cry. Since that discussion I have encountered many men in his position. They are lost and do not know what to do.

I picked him up one day for lunch after his classes. After some small talk, I asked about his childhood, which I found out was very rough. The things he had already experienced in his life were more than I could have imagined. He began to tell me about the emotional, verbal, and physical abuse he encountered at the hands of a relative. He told me story after story of nights where he would go hungry. He survived on small snacks throughout the day. Going without food for days was not abnormal for him. He had a part-time job, but most of his money was used for school. The experiences he told me about began to tear me to pieces. I had one thought—what if this was my son? I vowed that day to make sure his future was better than his past.

One thing he said during one of our many conversations that struck me were the words, "I feel intimidated." Those words reminded me of similar feelings in my past. I grew up in a very small town in Mississippi. The goal of many of my classmates was to work at the local furniture factory like their parents. Some had aspirations to work at the big bank on the corner. Some even aspired to work in the largest town about thirty minutes away. That was a big-time aspiration back then.

As for me, I did not know what I wanted to do. I did know I wanted something more out of life. I just did not know how to get it, and I was somewhat afraid to really reach out and explore because I was intimidated.

As a boy I felt intimidated to walk into the big bank on the corner. I felt like I was not good enough to be there. I just wanted to wear a nice suit like one of the men I saw working in the bank. I wanted to have a nameplate on a desk in my office. I loved the prestige of wearing a suit and exchanging pleasant conversation with customers. Being a bank officer looked appealing. My only problem was that I was too intimidated to ask for guidance on that career track. I felt the banking professionals were better than me because of what they appeared to have and what I did not have.

I lived in a doublewide trailer almost seven miles away from the town. There was a pond where I would go fishing and catch dinner for the evening. It was what I called "good country living." Although that was all I knew growing up, I wanted something more than that. I wanted to experience life outside of the routine I was accustomed to. I wanted to overcome intimidation and finally put on a suit.

That day came near my seventeenth birthday. I purchased my first suit. I wore that suit everywhere I possibly could. It became a symbol of my desire to conquer my intimidation.

I meet many men who feel intimidated by what they see and people they meet. I have even heard husbands say their wives intimidate them. And those who would not admit it, really do not need to because can be clear who has the upper hand. Some men feel their wives' education or accomplishments lower their value or position in the relationship if they don't have the same level of achievement. They are not mad. They are not angry. They are intimidated.

I had one husband tell me he felt like a hostage in his own home. His wife would hold her salary level over his head. She dictated his every move and limited the interaction he could have with his friends. She felt like she had the power to control him because she was the major breadwinner in the home.

A couple I advised many times was on the brink of divorce. I could not really put my finger on the root of their challenges even after talking on multiple occasions. The wife seemed very respectful and encouraging of her husband in public. There was not one time I ever witnessed his wife say something or do something that was derogatory. She served him like he was a king. In fact, many of the younger ladies at our church really admired her submission and love she showed her husband. Sadly enough, she could not get him to talk and express his feelings. She just kept finding herself with divorce papers being served to her, and she had run out of options. She did not want to divorce him.

I talked the husband into meeting with me after several refusals. We both shared a love for politics. He started poking at the food on his plate and began to zone out like he was in a trance. I asked him if there was something he wanted to say. Tears started to roll down his face. "Cornelius, my wife wears the pants in our house!" He excused himself to step away to compose himself. He did not want the other patrons to see him crying.

I inquired about his astonishing statement once he returned to the table. I told him about what I observed about his marriage. I told him how many people felt his wife treated him like a king and always spoke highly of him. I understand things are not always how they seem, so I wanted to know if it was genuine. If not, she was a great actress. The husband told me everything I observed about his marriage was right. His wife did treat him like a king. She made sure a hot meal was prepared nightly. She encouraged him daily. She spoke highly of him in public. He said his wife never made him feel less than a man.

I was confused after hearing all of this. I could not understand why he wanted to get a divorce. He said it was not another woman or man. He said his wife's higher paycheck made him feel like he was less than a man. His wife did not hold it over his head. She did not make him feel less than a man because of it. He felt that way. He felt too embarrassed to talk about it with her. He felt intimidated by the situation, so he chose not to raise the issue with his wife.

Like other men, his silence communicated something much larger than just a prideful ego as some would assume. I have heard women say that men need to just get over it and drop their macho ego. While there is some truth to it, it is not easy for men to just drop their desire to want to be the provider and caretaker for their family.

This man, like other men, had a bruised ego. A man with a bruised ego can say few words, but the words he does share can be demeaning and sarcastic. I understand a man's desire to be the breadwinner. We have a natural desire to provide for our family, and oftentimes, men gauge success by points. Men whose wives earn more money than them feel lost. I have known some men to get two or three jobs just to compensate for what they lack financially in comparison to their wives. Society can try to paint it as an ego problem, and I would not totally disagree. However, we cannot neglect the natural desire men have to provide and, ultimately, win the game. The husband and I talked for hours about his situation. I encouraged him not to look at his wife's income like it was any different.

The husband finally sat down with his wife to discuss how their salary differences were taking a toll on his self-esteem. His wife was nothing but encouraging to him. She helped him gain perspective, and communicated the same message about being on the same team that I communicated to him just days before.

Men must understand that the 'point system' many live by must be looked at from a healthier perspective. In marriage, a husband and wife are on the same team. That means that each basket she scores works towards the final score. When she wins, he wins! When teammates have different goals, the team suffers and a divided team is one that is sure to lose.

I know there are some wives who use their higher earnings to emasculate or imprison their husband. In this case, the wife makes it seem like they are not on the same team. Each time she does it, she castrates him. If he does not run, he will stay and grow silent. His silence will become resentment and guilt. He will be physically present, but mentally absent.

I encourage men in that situation to sit and talk with their wives. Tell her how she emasculates you each time she uses her money as a whip to keep you in line. Tell her how you feel enslaved. Confess to her that you are beginning to resent her because of her actions. If that does not work, I encourage you to seek out a counselor to mediate the discussion and raise issues that you may not be able to say in private.

Remember that God controls the game. Do not think for a second that one person's ability to score more points makes him or her any better than another. That is a sure way to fall. Do not ever think that a job, which can be lost at any moment, makes you any better than anyone else.

Money was the main cause for another couple's marital problems. The wife had the higher salary and flaunted that in front of her husband. Although she was repentant in my office, she continued her assault against him. About two weeks after the meeting in my office, I received a call from the husband. He told me his wife lost her job. She was the vice president of a start-up company in the greater Atlanta area. She was making well over six figures a year with a great benefits package. The CEO of the company called her into his office to let her know that they were making drastic cuts. She was being laid off with small severance package. She was distraught and hesitant to tell her husband because of the way she treated him. He worked as an accountant for a major finance firm in the greater Atlanta area. He reached out to me get advice on how to respond to her situation.

I advised him to encourage her and treat her the way he wanted to be treated in that situation. Instead of pulling back and making his wife feel miserable he decided to use this situation to get their attention back to where it was supposed to be—on God. They stopped keeping their money separate. They became fully transparent about what was going on in their accounts. He even created an account she could access to spend money as she pleased. Months later, he was shocked to find out that she saved a lot of the money in her account to buy him the motorcycle he had wanted for years. Their marriage is much stronger than ever. Sadly, it took her losing her job to humble her. She has since started her own company with her husband. He runs the financial side of the business, and she takes care of all administration. They are doing very well right now, and they help other married couples who have experienced corporate downsizing.

Another scenario I've seen is where the husband is in school while the wife works. Some think this is a backwards model. I have to disagree. Education is as valuable as employment and in fact, gives some advantage in the job-seeking process.

Although education does not always guarantee more money, it is very useful. Often a husband can feel uncomfortable with going to school and watching the children while his wife work to support his education. There is no reason to feel that way. Again this husband and wife are on the same team. I would just encourage any man in that situation to make sure he does not make himself a burden on anyone. That means he needs to go the extra mile to make sure he provides in the ways he has committed to. I know men in that situation who drive taxis in the morning, go to classes, and are back home in time to pick up the children and have family time.

If you find yourself in any of these situations, do not feel embarrassed. You are not alone. Do not grow silent. You may think your silence is better than expressing how you truly feel. Being silent is internalizing anger. You do not want to grow to resent your wife. I know God created us to be providers, but you must remember that God is our ultimate provider. Continue to pour your heart out to Him and let Him know how you feel about your circumstances. It could very well be a process you need to go through to learn humility. It sure taught me when I went through it.

Do not let your insecurities cause you to shrink away in embarrassment. Rest assured that God is able to heal you of any hurts you may have experienced because of emasculating comments about your lack of finances. Ultimately, you are not the money you make! Money should never define you. It is only a tool used to exchange one commodity for another. You must take control of your emotions in this area or it will control you.

Always remember that intimidation is perceived fear. It gives one the idea of being in danger of losing something or someone. Do not forget that God did not give you a fear of man of what he or she will do to you. If you have felt intimidated, go to God in prayer and ask Him to remove the fear. Then do everything in your power to develop within the situation. Do not be intimidated any longer.

Chapter 19

The Strong, Silent Type

My father is a truly a man of few words. I joke sometimes saying that I did not know he knew how to talk until I was six-years-old. I have always looked at him as being the strong, silent type—a man of few words. He speaks through his silence with resolve and power. This character type can command attention just by entering a room. It is impossible for many of them to go unnoticed.

Many of these men are not silent because they have nothing to say; many are silent because they want to make sure what they have to say is worth saying. They need a reason and a purpose to speak. They do not talk and share their feelings indiscriminately. They do not have to sound dominant or overbearing. Many people think these men are the most difficult to understand. These men are usually very straightforward when people do hear them speak. They will tell you what they have to tell you when they want to tell you.

My grandfather was one of those men. I do not know much

about him. He died when I was six, but I have some very fond memories of time with him. We would ride in his pickup truck through the town without saying a word. It really made every word he spoke extra special. It was like he was reserving every word for the right moment. I had no other choice but to listen each time he spoke. It was like the clouds opened up and trumpets began to sound. His presence was captivating. All I wanted from him was his approval. I was drawn to his strength, and his silence intrigued me. I always wondered what he was thinking, but I did not want to ask.

One thing I began to recognize about strong, silent men is that their quiet strength does not mean they are not reachable. I grew up thinking my grandfather was immortal. It crushed me when I found out he died of a blood clot. I thought he was invisible. His death was a wakeup call to mortality.

The truth is that strong, silent types are not always strong. They have weaknesses. They have needs, too. They need someone to confide in. They need someone help them. They need a shoulder to lean on. They need ways to cope with the stresses of life.

For many strong, silent types, their strength becomes their greatest weakness. They mistakenly assume they are strong enough to handle life alone. They try to become an island to themselves. They think their strength will be their shield. Many of them spend their lives providing solutions for everyone around them. They are the strength for their family, friends, and community. They cannot handle sickness or weakness that doesn't have a cure or provide a solution. Carrying the weight of fear and sickness can cause some individuals to stop living even before they actually die.

Silence is not always a bad thing. Many men use silence as a means of collecting their thoughts. This allows them to think before they speak. They search for things that are reasonable and appropriate. Silence does shut others out. While people in their lives may mistake the silence for being distant, they are really thinking so they can have something worth saying.

My wife had to figure this out about me. I used silence as a means of thinking through things. On the other hand, my wife wanted to talk about everything. I wanted and needed time and silence to process my thoughts before speaking. My silence was never intended to irritate my wife. Sometimes it would take me days to return to a topic we had been discussing. She did not understand why I needed to think before speaking. In her mind the two things—thinking and speaking—were inseparable. Coming to an understanding about this really helped our marriage.

I can recall when I was in high school and being considered for a six-week honors program. It was something I really wanted to do. I had to take an IQ test, write an essay, be nominated by two different teachers and go through three different interview sessions. I was nominated in the area of social studies. I felt like I breezed through the first set of interviews. The first one was a one-on-one interview. The second one was an interview by a group of advisors from all over the state of Georgia. I felt like I passed those interviews with flying colors. The last interview was difficult. It was a group interview. There I was in a room with eleven other students from around the state. They were the smartest students in the field of social studies in the state of Georgia. I did not feel like I was supposed to be in the same room with them. I sat there the entire time in complete silence.

Many people assume I am extroverted because I am a pastor. In actuality, I prefer to be out of the spotlight. I will not talk unless I feel like I have something to say, and I did not say much the entire time I was in that group of young people. A few of the students approached me. They questioned why I was not saying anything. "Who do you think you are sitting there saying nothing? You just sat there and judged all of us as if you were someone special. You really think you are better than us, don't you?" I was shocked! I could not understand how they could assume all of that because of my silence. It took time for me to realize that my silence made me appear distant. My body language showed them that I was very much engaged in conversation. I was leaning forward. I was listening intently. But I did not say much. They took my silence as disrespect. That was not how I meant for it to be perceived.

Truthfully, I felt like I was in an uncomfortable situation. I felt like everyone in the room was far more advanced than I. I felt like everyone had something much more valuable to say. Silence was my only way of not revealing my true feelings.

Many of the strong, silent types are just shy, uncomfortable, or frustrated. Many times this frustration comes when they are being asked to share their feelings or emotions. This can make others uncomfortable to be around them because their silence brings a certain awkwardness that some people do not want to deal with.

The strong, silent type has been the main character on the big screen. Characters like James Bond or roles played by actors like Clint Eastwood have helped to shape the view of the strong, silent type. These men had authority in their voice, were not afraid to fight, and were willing to live in dangerous situations. One key aspect we fail to understand about these men is they are fictitious. What the movies failed to show are their moments of desperation and sadness. It portrays them as strong, valiant, and resourceful. They are portrayed as the face of the alpha male.

My wife and I have sat down with many women who thought they were marrying Mr. Tall, Dark, and Handsome only to find out he is really Mr. Strong and Silent. I would highly recommend not pressing the strong, silent type about what he is thinking. I always felt like I would tell my wife what I was thinking if I felt like she needed to know. Is that reasonable? No, not always. Nevertheless, I would encourage those who are trying to decode the strong and silent man's language to focus on what he does instead of constantly focusing on what he is not saying or asking what he is thinking.

I also encourage you not to assume he does not want to talk to you just because he does not want to express his feelings. Communicating how one feels is not always easy. What you perceive as simple and easy is not the same for everyone else. Do not try to change him. I am a firm believer that only God has the ability to change a man. The strong, silent type is usually a loner. He is not necessarily excited about hanging out with a crowd. When a wife is a social butterfly and keeps a calendar full of events, dragging her strong, silent husband to her various engagements could end up being a frustrating experience for both of them.

The silent man will talk; he just has to make sure he has something worth saying. He has to make sure he has time, trust, and respect. Those are three necessities for him to open up and talk. He may just need time to warm up.

My wife always says that she searches for the off button to hush me up when I start talking. She does not understand how someone who does not always talk has so much to say. I think it makes perfect sense. Since I do not talk often, when I chose to, there is a lot to say. So when I talk, prepare yourself for an avalanche of conversation. The same may be true for the strong, silent man in your life.

Be sensitive to his silence. And be patient with him. He needs a conversationalist and someone to express her feelings to him. Your willingness to communicate serves as an open door to encourage him to talk more. I can guarantee that I communicate a lot more often now than when I was first married. I have grown to enjoy conversing. The strong, silent man in your life will learn to like it as well.

After Heather and I were married, I shared how she could help me learn how to communicate better.

1. I asked her to be patient with me. I was not going to change overnight.
2. I asked her specific questions, not open-ended ones. Open-ended questions usually mean I have to speak until I discover the answer she is looking for me to give. That can be exhausting.
3. I asked her to gently challenge me to talk in an encouraging way so that I'd be more willing to open up about things I would normally suppress.
4. I asked her to prepare me for the kind of conversation she wants to have. For example, would our talk be about exploring feelings or would the tone be more confrontational? Would she be seeking solutions or just have a need to vent? Those answers help me know if I should plan to only listen as a sounding board or listen to provide a solution. Zeroing in on the nature of our conversations helps both of us communicate effectively. I know my wife well enough now that I can tell the kind of conversation she wants—sometimes by a facial expression, the inflection in her voice, or other triggers.
5. Lastly, I asked her to respect my space. I know this can sound crass. I am married, right? I do not have space, right? Well, that is not totally true. There are times when because of my level of fatigue or involvement in a project knowing the kind of

conversation she wants, helps me to mentally prepare to be productively engaged with her. She deserves my undivided attention, and nothing less. I cannot give her that if I am mentally and physically exhausted. I do not want to give her the crumbs of my day. My wife is a wise woman. She makes sure there is at least one day on my calendar that is designated for a lunch or dinner date for just the two of us. We take a sabbatical from work to entertain one another. We go away so we can free our minds of everything else and focus on another. This gives us an opportunity to connect and communicate without any distractions.

I hope these ideas can help female readers understand the strong, silent type of man in their lives and help him communicate a little better. Just remember that he is a work-in-progress. His physical stature and tough demeanor does not mean he does not need help, encouragement, patience or support. Your greatest work is to pray for him and encourage him.

Chapter 20

No Lost Opportunities

"Will everyone please stand as I read from the Book of John, chapter 14?" asked the preacher as he stood in front of the casket. The mourners for the deceased family member trailed them.

The funeral service had begun. As family and friends walked around to view the deceased, one of the aunts broke into tears. This brought immediate sadness to everyone in the congregation. Then the deceased's daughter let out a blood-curdling scream that could be heard from outside the sanctuary. The daughter threw herself over the casket and began to cry. Her screams grew louder and louder. She was her daddy's little girl, and his death would leave a big hole in her heart.

The deceased's son sat there on the front row almost motionless. He was doing everything he could to hold back the tears. His heart was heavy. He and his father argued just five years to the very day of his death. They had not spoken since. The argument was not worth remembering. He had so much to tell his deceased father, but time had run out. He kept telling himself that he would talk with him at some point. He kept putting it off. Now it was too late. He lost the opportunity to tell his father how much he truly appreciated him and to ask for forgiveness for disrespecting him and his house. But the opportunity was lost.

How often do we hear that we need to tell people how we truly feel about them before they die? I know I have heard it many times, yet it does not cause me to open up and communicate. I have watched as many of my loved ones were put in the ground. Their lives were cut short, and I continued to put off talking to them because I felt like I had time.

A cousin of mine whom I considered a brother started to get involved with the wrong set of friends. We were childhood friends who had become so bonded that he was the closest I ever came to having a blood brother. There were times when he was my only friend.

We both attended the same high school, and we were in the same grade and were supposed to graduate in May 2004. In September 2003, my cousin and I got into an argument on our way to work. He talked about needing a gun, and I disagreed with him. I did not like the crowd he was starting to hang around. I voiced my frustrations with him, and we both said some really awful things to one another. I told him I would never speak to him again and that the gun would be the death of him one day. I did not think anything of it on that day. He went his way, and I went mine.

It was February 2004 and I was at a party. My mom called me and told me to come home. She just felt something was not right—her discerning mother's intuition. After getting in the bed and sleeping for what felt like ten minutes, my sister opened my door and said, "He's been shot!" My cousin had been shot. We rushed to the downtown Atlanta hospital where he was taken. He was already dead when we arrived. There was nothing the doctors could do. The bullet pierced his heart.

I did not want to be around anyone that night. All I could think about was the argument we had a couple of months prior to his death. I felt like I had given up on my cousin. I let him go to the wolves alone. It took years for me to forgive myself for the words we exchanged during our argument. I have finally let it all go. The fact of the matter was that my cousin was dead.

I wrestled with deciding on attending my cousin's funeral. It was taking place on the day that I was to compete in a mock trial competition. I was the captain of the team and I was the lead defense. We had all been practicing and rehearsing everything since the beginning of the school year. I did not want to let my fellow teammates down, and I did not want to let my family down.

To compromise, my entire mock trial team took a bus to attend the wake and say our final goodbyes. As I walked in the funeral home, my knees began to weaken. I was starting to lose my balance. As I walked up to the casket, I completely blacked out. When I came to I was sitting on a bench in front of the body with a cold towel on my forehead. Tears would not come. The regret I felt was excruciating. I was tormented with the fact that I missed an opportunity to tell him how I felt. I missed an opportunity to tell him I was sorry for my actions and for leaving him alone. I missed an opportunity to be the brother to him that he was to me for so many years.

I do not fully know what it is about men that causes us not to say what we should and what we need to say when the opportunity is presented to us. Some of us don't recognize opportunities. However, we can create the opportunities if we truly believe it is important.

I want to challenge the men reading this book to express themselves verbally. We must live in the moment. We cannot allow our silence to cause us to miss the opportunities we are given in life to speak. Oftentimes we think things, but we do not say them. Perhaps we think what we have to say is not worth hearing or that those who are supposed to hear it will not receive it.

I know there have been many things I have wanted to say to my wife, but there have been times when I felt like she would not receive what I had to say. I was robbing her of an opportunity to hear what was on my heart. I was robbing her of the opportunity to tell her how I truly felt about her or about something that happened. Instead of speaking, I stayed silent.

There have also been times where I have said something about my wife to someone else, but I did not say it to her. For example, I would tell one of my friends about the great things my wife has done, but I would not tell her those things as we lay beside one another in bed. It makes no sense to withhold encouragement from those we love, but we have all done it. Our silence cripples our ability to truly express how we feel. I would like to think that although I do not say it, my actions are communicating my feelings.

I want to challenge you to be more verbal. I know that can be difficult for some. I know because it has been challenging for me. It took me some time to finally open up to my wife and tell her about the peak and pit of my day, something she enjoys doing around the dinner table.

One would think that those who make a living speaking and writing, as I do, would not find it difficult to be open and verbal, but that is not the case. I can write books all day long. I can stand up and preach all day long. But it can be difficult to open my mouth and express what is really going on in my heart.

I have had far too many opportunities where I was burying loved ones without telling them how I truly felt about them. I kept putting it off for another day. It is arrogant of me to assume that I will have the opportunity to do tomorrow what I know I should do today. I do not want you to live regretting what you should have said, but didn't.

You must take advantage of every opportunity you are given. Do not assume you have tomorrow. It is not promised to us. Express your love right now. Give the flowers right now. Go out on the date right now. Pour out your heart right now. Do not put it off.

Never forget that coffins cannot hear anything. You cannot communicate what is on your heart after the person is gone. I have encountered far too many divorced couples who regret their decision to divorce. They have grown and matured. They have gotten to a point where they finally want to be a wife or a husband. They finally want to be selfless. They finally want to give the flowers, go on the dates, or take the long walks, listen as the spouse talks about his/her day and kiss one another goodnight. I have met far too many fathers who want to turn back the hands of time to be the fathers their children deserved instead of putting other things before them.

One father expressed his frustration to me when he realized his son felt separated from him. The father realized he put his job over his son. He was never able to make it to his son's sporting events. His job demanded so much from him. He found it difficult to balance his work and home life. The father finally became vice president of the company. He was making more money than he ever made before. He was finally sitting in the corner office. It seemed like everything was going as planned. He was on top of the world. That was until he went to the company's holiday party. The Chief Executive Officer's son came to introduce his father to speak. After an engaging introduction, the son asked everyone in the audience this question, "What would your child have to say about you if he had to introduce you to the world?" Those words pierced the new vice president's heart. He did not feel like his son would have the most glowing remarks about him.

In an effort to make up for lost time, the father bought his son all the sports equipment he had longed for. His son's reaction to all the new gifts was, "It's a little too late for that stuff, dad. I dropped sports years ago. I love science! You wouldn't know that though because you are never around."

The father was trying to build a relationship and do things he thought his son would appreciate. Unfortunately, he was basing his obligation as father on what he once knew about his son, not all he should have currently known about his son. The father's actions were based in the past, not the present. He missed the opportunities to hit the ball with his son. He missed the opportunities to throw the football. His son had simply outgrown those interests.

I think about the time when my son was born. I did not want to regret missing any opportunities. I was there when he was born. I was there to hold him the first night. I was there to change his first diaper. I was there when he said his first word. I was there when he started walking. I did not want to miss the opportunities. Childhood flies like lightning. Opportunities to enjoy milestones are priceless and irreplaceable. Each day is a gift, and I cannot afford to ignore those times with him.

To my female readers, I encourage you to do four things.

First, pray for your man. Pray that God will soften his heart and give him the desire to communicate with you. Pray that God will show you areas of your life that need to be changed that might facilitate conversation.

Secondly, ask questions. Do not assume or doubt him. Ask questions to get information. Do not convict him before he has been given a chance to state his case. Ask questions to allow him to talk about what is on his heart. Give him the opportunity to respond. But do not ever assume he is thinking one way or another. Assuming will place you in a position where you start building a case based on what you think, not what you know.

Thirdly, focus on what he is not saying if he is not opening up. Study his actions. Encourage him to take time away and relax together. Encourage him to unplug from his daily activities so he can think. Encourage him to associate with mature, wise men who can encourage and guide him. Encourage him to do things he will enjoy.

Fourthly, rely on the Holy Spirit for guidance. Ask the Holy Spirit to give you wisdom on how to communicate with your loved one. Ask Him to tell you when to speak and when not to speak. He will guide you.

To my male readers, I encourage you to do one thing—open up your mouth and speak. If you are like me, you may be thinking about all the reasons you should stay silent. At one time, I felt that way. I had my many reasons as well, so I know how you feel. However, I found out I had to open up and express what was in my heart. I had to do it for the health of my marriage, for the growth of my relationship with my children, and for the betterment of my friendships. My church deserves to be led by a healthy pastor who does not miss an opportunity to be appreciative and open about what is in my heart. Your family deserves a healthy and communicative father, grandfather, great grandfather, son, nephew, uncle or cousin. Find ways to communicate how you feel.

It is safe to assume, with this my eighth book, that writing is one form of communication that I enjoy. Others may like to write music or sing. Some may choose spoken word or poetry as their platform. You may like to just sit down and talk in a safe, comfortable environment. Wherever you feel most comfortable, communicate!

If communication continues to be a challenge, would recommend speaking with a wise, mature, and Spirit-filled advisor who can help guide you in the right direction. Use wisdom before you speak. The goal is not to say everything that comes to your mind. A fool speaks because he wants to just say something; a wise man speaks because what he has to say is worth saying.

I encourage you to begin small. Communication can be very intimidating for some. It can seem nearly impossible for others. You are capable of doing it. You can open your mouth and begin to confess what is on your heart. You are capable of using wisdom to discern what needs to be said.

Make communication simple. Start the day with "Good morning." Close the day with "Good night." Make time in your day to talk to your family about their day, their issues, their concerns, and their successes. Go prepared to listen. Then respond when you have something worth saying.

Pride will keep your mouth closed. It will intimidate you and make you think the task of communication is too big for you. Do not fall for the enemy's lie. And do not think that your inability to verbally express yourself makes you imperfect. Start the process today. Take time to unplug from social media. Contact and connect with those you love and tell them how you truly feel about them. Write letters. Send emails. Make phone calls. Plan a lunch together. Make your expressions personal. Create opportunities to tell people how you truly feel about them while they can hear you. You never know when that opportunity will be taken away. Do not waste it!

Now is your time, strong and silent man to share your words of wisdom, love, insight, compassion, and blessing. Let your tongue be like the pen of a ready writer... and *speak*!

21818104R00123

Made in the USA
San Bernardino, CA
08 June 2015